Praise for *Navigating Your Child's Unique Mental & Physical Needs*

"As a therapist working with families for more than 30 years and, myself, a former Clinical Director in a special education school, I happily recommend Dr. McGrady's book as a treasure chest for parents. This book takes you by the hand, explains, encourages, and educates every step of the way as parents navigate the space between their child's emerging needs and the services of the educational system.

The detailed and specific information about what school systems offer is carefully and respectfully woven into a context of empathy and consideration for children and families. Dr. McGrady's knowledge is exceptional, and the way she presents information makes for a very engaging read that imparts tremendous wisdom. I have many books on my professional shelves, but only a select few get dog-eared from frequent referencing. This will be one of those books."

~ **Kathleen Landers**, LCSW-C, Founding Director of Sequence Services

"This parent's guide to navigating the unique mental and physical needs of children takes the mystery out of supporting children who need extra support, so they can thrive within their educational environments. I recommend this book to any parent who needs guidance on how to best advocate for their child's unique educational needs."

~ **Dr. Camille Bryant**, professor and mother of two

I0809126

"As a parent of a child with special needs, I'm quite familiar with feeling 'misunderstood, uncertain, overwhelmed, or alone,' as Dr. McGrady describes in this unique and beneficial guide for forming school and parental partnerships. Putting the parents at the helm, this book serves as a map for navigating partnerships with a child's school system to ensure the best possible educational outcomes. Between therapists, administrators, assessments, and other appointments, parents are inundated with acronyms, such IEP, IFSP, and IDEA. However, Dr. McGrady offers easily understood, comprehensive definitions while walking you through the entire educational process; therefore, empowering parents with a sense of control in an otherwise uncontrollable diagnosis.

Whether your child has a physical, mental, or learning disability (or a combination of these), the book begins with the data gathering step via your child's teacher, school psychologist, pediatrician, and extended family caregivers, then moves on to the evaluation process. The discussion then moves to accepting and embracing a diagnosis and building a blueprint for treatment. Dr. McGrady includes important questions for parents to ask during school meetings and how to create a long-lasting, positive relationship with the entire school staff. Once again, this guide is for supporting you: the most important person in your child's life."

~ **Jacqueline Renfrow**, education commissioner and mother of three

"The author's tone is empathetic as she highlights practical strategies for parents and guardians of students with a mental or physical disability. The book features a detailed table of contents and succinct summaries of each chapter in the front, so readers can quickly and easily find the necessary information. Navigating the numerous processes that often accompany the identification of a disability can be overwhelming and confusing for families. I highly recommend this text as it was written in a way that aims to validate and empower adults as they seek resources for their student inside and outside of school."

~ **Dr. Jennifer Snow**, assistant professor and former high school teacher

Navigating Your Child's Unique Mental & Physical Needs

A Parent's Guide to School Supports

Also from the Boys Town Press

Common Sense Parenting®

Common Sense Parenting of Toddlers and Preschoolers

Mental Health: From Diagnosis to Delivery

Building Resiliency in Youth

Building Resiliency in Children

Building Resiliency in Teens

Youth Resources

My Anxiety Is Messing Things Up

Why Is Drama Always Following Me?

Am I Weird?

Managing Sadness

Middle School Misfits

The Good, the Bad, and the Backstory

Molly and the Runaway Trolley

Awesome Dawson Has Big Emotions

Navigating Your Child's Unique Mental & Physical Needs

A Parent's Guide to School Supports

BOYS TOWN Press

Boys Town, Nebraska

KAT McGRADY, EdD, LCPC, NCC

Navigating Your Child's Unique Mental & Physical Needs

Published by Boys Town Press
Father Flanagan's Boys' Home
Boys Town, NE 68010

ISBN: 979-8-88907-022-1

Boys Town Press is the publishing division of Boys Town, a national organization serving children and families.

Publisher's Cataloging-in-Publication Data

Names: McGrady, Kat, author.

Title: Navigating your child's unique mental & physical needs : a parent's guide to school supports / Kat McGrady. EdD, LCPC, NCC.

Description: Boys Town, NE : Boys Town Press, [2025] | Includes index.

Identifiers: ISBN: 979-8-88907-022-1

Subjects: LCSH: Children with disabilities--Education--Handbooks, manuals, etc. | Children with disabilities--Mental health--Handbooks, manuals, etc. | Children with autism spectrum disorders--Education--Handbooks, manuals, etc. | Children with autism spectrum disorders --Mental health--Handbooks, manuals, etc. | Children with attention-deficit hyperactivity disorder--Education--Handbooks, manuals, etc. | Children with attention-deficit hyperactivity disorder--Mental health--Handbooks, manuals, etc. | Special education-- Handbooks, manuals, etc. | Parents of children with disabilities--Handbooks, manuals, etc. | BISAC: FAMILY & RELATIONSHIPS / Autism Spectrum Disorders. | FAMILY & RELATIONSHIPS / Attention Deficit Disorder (ADD-ADHD) | FAMILY & RELATIONSHIPS / Children with Special Needs. | PSYCHOLOGY / Mental Health.

Classification: LCC: LC4031 .M34 2025 | DDC: 371.9/0973--dc23

10 9 8 7 6 5 4 3 2 1

Table of Contents

Downloadable Tools and Checklists

ACCESS:
https://www.boystownpress.org/book-downloads

ENTER:
Your first and last names
Email address
Code: **88907pgs s0221**
Check yes to receive emails to ensure your email link is received.

Introduction

A RIDDLE:
What do the following children have in common?

Fatima, Age 6

Fatima comes from a middle-class background. She currently lives with her parents, two siblings, and her beloved cat in the suburbs of Oklahoma City. Fatima attends an award-winning public school. Her mother is a middle school administrator, and her father holds an honorable position in the military. Fatima and her family relocated to the States last year. Previously, she attended American School while her father completed his station overseas. Fatima adores Taylor Swift, as well as drawing anime, eating pizza, and spending time with her friends.

Toby, Age 12

Toby comes from a socioeconomic background marked by insecurity. After a series of unfortunate events, Toby was sent to live with his aunt and older cousin in Baltimore's urban core. He attends a charter school noted for its low achievement scores. His aunt is the sole financial provider. Toby loves gaming, playing lacrosse, and creating, illustrating, and narrating superhero stories written by his cousin.

Lily, Age 16

Lily hails from an upper-class background. The adopted daughter of diplomats, she lives in rural Virginia and attends a prestigious private school. In her free time, Lily enjoys horseback riding, ballet, texting with friends (phone and video calls aren't as enjoyable), and binge watching the latest and greatest shows.

Christian, Age 2

Christian is the youngest son in a middle-class family. Residing in a quiet neighborhood just outside of Charleston, South Carolina, he attends nursery school and belongs to the local infants and toddlers program. Christian's parents are business owners and first-generation immigrants. Christian enjoys dinosaur toys, cuddles, swimming, and being read to by his parents and older siblings.

ANSWER:
Each one is living with a disability or a condition that impacts their daily lives.

Disabilities and conditions that impact children can include mental health issues, learning challenges, physical restrictions, or a combination of all three. These disabilities and conditions can vary in terms of magnitude, symptoms, and the demographic makeup of those impacted.

A lack of knowledge and awareness about childhood disabilities, how those disabilities present themselves, the similarity of symptoms between comparable conditions, and a child's ability to conceal or compensate for their condition can lead to misinterpretations and incorrect treatment.

Without answers or proper support, a childhood disability can seem like an impossible obstacle to overcome. As a loving parent, you may feel like an invisible island, thinking no one can see you, hear you, or relate to your struggles. However, if your child has a diagnosed disability, you most certainly are not alone. According to the National Center for Education Statistics (NCES), more than seven million public school students received special education services as recently as the mid-2020s.[1] In addition, more than one million students qualified for a Section 504 Plan as of the mid-2000s.[2]

The following pages offer a blueprint you can follow to navigate the special education process. Each chapter highlights key elements, such as recognizing possible disabilities or conditions, the evaluation and assessment process, diagnosis, and treatment planning. In addition, there is an abundance of useful information, based on research and authentic parent experiences, which can support you throughout the diagnostic and treatment planning process.

What to Expect in Each Chapter

Learning occurs when new information connects to and builds upon previously acquired knowledge. As such, the chapters are formatted to connect and build on each other.

CHAPTER 1 includes a brief overview of the history behind treatment plans in America's educational system. To ensure you gain a solid foundational understanding of how treatment plans have changed throughout the years and where they may be going in the future, this chapter outlines major laws and landmark decisions. The chapter also takes a more in-depth look at the current state of mental health, behavioral health, and learning disabilities in our nation.

CHAPTER 2 defines and distinguishes between the main types of disorders that qualify for a treatment plan. Potential indicators of a disability or condition that may be observed during your child's developmental stages, along with the causes and dangers of self-diagnosis and parental misdiagnosis, are highlighted. Suggestions on how to discuss a self-diagnosis with your child and how to avoid mislabeling or misdiagnosing your child are included. The chapter also offers examples and ideas for gathering data if you suspect your child may have a disorder.

CHAPTER 3 expands on the steps you can take if a disability or condition is likely. Suggestions on who to reach out to and the types of data to collect and share

are explained. Additionally, the chapter explores how to develop and implement a data collection plan and how to distinguish between the main types of treatment plans. Various elements of treatment plans, including what to expect, supporting roles and their tasks, and mandates tied to each type of plan, are highlighted.

CHAPTER 4 identifies the differences between school-based versus private testing and their pros and cons. Recommendations on how to choose an evaluator, what to expect during the evaluation process, and possible steps to take if a private evaluation does not seem financially feasible are outlined. In addition, recommendations on maximizing the benefits of an evaluation report are included. A comparison of educational advocates and special education attorneys, including roles and goals, is explained. The chapter also examines when and how to work with an advocate or attorney, questions to ask to ensure you are choosing the right support for your unique needs, and what to do if you cannot afford an advocate or attorney.

CHAPTER 5 provides guidance on acknowledging, accepting, and embracing your child's diagnosis. Helpful tips on processing and coping with your child's diagnosis and empowering your child to confidently explore and better understand their diagnosis are included. Tips on supporting nondisabled siblings and encouraging a strengthened family unit by embracing and working with the diagnosis also are shared.

CHAPTER 6 lays out a step-by-step guide on what to do before, during, and after an initial treatment planning meeting. Suggestions on how to develop the most effective and comprehensive plan for your child are included. The chapter also highlights general timelines for key deadlines in an Individualized Education Plan (IEP)/504 Plan, from referral to treatment plan implementation.

CHAPTER 7 examines how to maintain an effective partnership with your child's school and other key players. Included are themes surrounding team dynamics and cultural considerations, how to respond if a treatment plan is not being followed, and steps to take if your child is not receiving mandated free and appropriate education.

CHAPTER 8 is dedicated to the importance of your roles and responsibilities. Recognizing common worries, managing emotions, understanding your child's needs, and maintaining your physical and emotional well-being are covered. The chapter ends with helpful definitions and explanations of acronyms that are commonly heard in most treatment planning meetings.

1. National Center for Education Statistics. (2023). Students With Disabilities. *Condition of Education*. U.S. Department of Education, Institute of Education Sciences. Retrieved from https://nces.ed.gov/programs/coe/indicator/cgg.
2. Civil Rights Data Collection Office for Civil Rights (OCR) (2018). *2017-2018 State and National Tables*. U.S. Department of Education, Office for Civil Rights. https://civilrightsdata.ed.gov/estimations/2017-2018.

CHAPTER 1

Treatment Plans in America's Educational System

As a parent, you want to provide your child with the tools necessary to reach their life goals. You may teach them manners, morals, and what it means to be a good human. You may show them they are loved and valued by showing up and being present, nurturing, and encouraging. You may teach them life skills or introduce them to coaches, educators, and mentors who will enrich their lives. No matter how you do it, you invest your time, energy, love, and knowledge into helping your child find success. While these acts undoubtedly launch your child in a positive direction, additional or more adapted levels of support may be needed if they are to reach their full potential.

This is particularly true when looking at the challenges facing our youngest generation and how those challenges are impacting them. While it is true that the needs of young people can often shift and sway with the times and tides, there are new factors at play that are contributing to these shifts. Some of these key influences include:

- **Societal and cultural events.** Young people are molded by their surroundings, lifestyle, and exposure to experiences. For this reason, societal and cultural events play a major role in issues related to anxiety, resilience, and emotional and behavioral regulation. These events not only impact the social, emotional, and mental health of youth, they also can create larger learning gaps in vulnerable and high-risk populations.[1] In other words, major events within a child's life can impact their overall success.

  While every generation has faced its own struggles and every child has faced some form of adversity, today's youth are dealing with pressures that are broader, more pervasive, and often more intense. Can you think of any potential ways your child has been affected by social and cultural events (the pandemic and post-pandemic life, political polarization, climate change concerns, multiple ongoing wars, gun violence, school violence, self-identity as it relates to gender, race, and sexuality)? Does your child have unrestricted or unfiltered access to information about these topics – information that may not be age appropriate?

- **Technological advances.** I can see your head nodding in agreement about this one. This very topic is probably one that you have discussed repeatedly with your child, partner, and other parents: what to do about all these devices?! Our kids are becoming exposed to the positives and negatives of digital technology at an earlier age. We can all agree there are some astonishing positives that come with technology. But, many argue, access, exposure, and reliance on social media and gaming devices has led to a decline in the physical and mental health of many children and teens. Studies have linked the use of social media and long hours in front of a screen to higher rates of depression, anxiety, feelings of isolation, suicidal ideation, physical complications, and lack of sleep. On top of these increases, data suggests that social media usage and excessive screen time can lead to decreases in self-esteem, empathy, social skills, healthy identity development, and the ability to concentrate when offline.

- **Changes in the educational system.** Studies and experiences related to disabilities and conditions that can impact a child's success has led to a number of shifts in how educators and other stakeholders support students. As our understanding of children's needs and how those needs can best be met improves and expands, our ability to maximize our support for kids improves, too.
- **Research and diagnostic improvements.** Our understanding of disabilities and conditions that can impact a child's success is continuously advancing. In recent years, research has allowed us the ability to recognize and better understand various diagnoses, which has led to more awareness and, potentially, higher levels of diagnoses in young people.

There has been a sharp rise in requests for and application of supports for children in schools and beyond. Some think that an increased awareness of mental health and learning needs, reduced stigma surrounding these needs, and more openness toward seeking support have contributed to this rise. Others believe that distressing experiences, such as the pandemic and current societal tensions, are exaggerating issues and leading to misinterpretations about what our children actually need. Then, of course, there are those who believe there truly is a large rise in diagnosable conditions among our children.

There are a number of factors that can impact your child's academic, behavioral, and cognitive abilities. Whatever the causes may be, your child deserves an environment based in understanding, awareness, and collective support in order to overcome their challenges and embrace their own unique strengths.

FIGURE 1

Influences on Childhood Performance and Presentation

Biological	*Trauma*	*Negative self-image*
Lifestyle	*Environmental*	*Historical*
Social	*Genetics*	*Lack of supports*
Bullying	*Mindset*	*Socioeconomic*
Medical	*Brain makeup*	*ACES (Adverse Childhood Experiences)*

Without the proper roadmap, however, navigating the parenting journey with a child who requires a more tailored level of care can potentially lead you down a path littered with frustration and burnout. Oftentimes, parents of children with specific needs feel as if they are lone soldiers fighting an uphill battle. They feel as if no one understands their struggles parenting a child whose needs the parents *themselves* may not fully comprehend. Parents feel as if no one understands their child and, therefore, cannot see the amazing qualities they possess. They feel as if there are no effective systems or supports dedicated to helping their child reach their full potential.

If you feel misunderstood, uncertain, overwhelmed, or alone, know there is hope. While help and support may seem inaccessible or even nonexistent, there are, in fact, a number of brilliant and responsive resources available. Our nation's education system has put into place effective policies and safeguards to ensure positive outcomes for our children. These policies and safeguards are designed to ensure specific populations of students are provided care that is free from discrimination, unfairness, and any other unjust restrictions.

The more you become aware of what is out there, the more assurance you will have in knowing your child is seen and understood, you are seen and understood, and there are effective and intertwined systems in place to ensure your child reaches their full academic, emotional, and social potential. For example, you have the right to ask about safeguards, such as comprehensive treatment plans that follow specific protocols, to ensure your child receives a free and appropriate education. You also have the right to appeal decisions or advocate for more supports if you feel your child is not receiving what they need and deserve.

Familiarity with these supports and how to access them, though, is key. The following chapters outline the major resources and safeguards available to you and your child, as well as how to obtain them. In addition, you can read brief summaries of the landmark decisions and agencies which created these resources in the Appendix.

As you read, you may still feel somewhat confused about next steps. That's okay. Parenting today can be hard. Parenting a child who requires specific accommodations or modifications to thrive, especially if you are not sure how to provide those modifications, can be much harder. Use this book as a resource to improve your understanding, build your confidence, strengthen your resolve, and guide your child to success!

1. Colvin, M.K., Reesman, J., & Glen, T. (2022). Reforming learning disorder diagnosis following COVID-19 educational disruption. *Nature Reviews Psychology 1,* 251–252. https://doi.org/10.1038/s44159-022-00052-0.

CHAPTER 2

Diagnosis: Symptoms, Dangers, and Prevalence of Self-Diagnosis

Confirmation from a qualified professional that your child does indeed have a diagnosis can be both valuable and reassuring. A verified diagnosis brings with it a clearcut list of universally recognized symptoms and evidence-based treatment options.

Educating yourself on the particulars of your child's diagnosis can lead to a greater understanding of their needs and the supports that should be put in place. In addition, the ability to recognize how behaviors you observe align with the symptoms of a diagnosis can help you...

- Understand more completely your child's needs and shift your parenting techniques to meet those needs.
- Regain a sense of control in terms of knowing what your child needs, why they need it, and where to seek support when necessary.

- Build a stronger parent-child relationship based on empathy and awareness.
- Foster a deeper connection with your child.

Finally, obtaining an official diagnosis can empower your child by giving them a concrete name to explain the difficulties they may be experiencing. The more your child learns about their diagnosis, the more they will be able to recognize...

- Their symptoms are not character flaws or personal failures.
- There are ways to manage the symptoms.
- They are not alone in their experiences. (An official diagnosis means that these symptoms are experienced by others, and there are people working to help those who have gone through exactly what your child is experiencing.)

When your child understands the nature of their diagnosis, they can then be inspired to overcome it.

With that said, however, misdiagnoses, mislabeling, or failing to recognize when a diagnosis is present can lead to a number of unfavorable outcomes. For this reason, it's important to have an awareness of not only common disabilities and conditions in children, including possible symptoms and initial steps to take if you suspect a disability, but also the related causes, dangers, and preventative actions that can be taken to protect your child from a misdiagnosis or a mislabeling.

Learning Disabilities, Mental Health Conditions, and Physical Disabilities Defined

The Americans with Disabilities Act defines an individual with a disability as "a person who has a physical or mental impairment that substantially limits one or more major life activities, a person who has a history or record of such an impairment, or a person who is perceived by others as having such an impairment."[1] This can include learning disabilities, mental health conditions, or physical disabilities.

Although these three categories fall under the umbrella classification of disability, there are substantial differences among the three. These differences require their own unique modifications and accommodations to ensure that education is fair and appropriate for everyone, regardless of disability or special needs. This is important because it demonstrates our education system's recognition that...

1. Each child matters.
2. Each child's education matters.
3. Each child's future matters.
4. Each child is capable of doing amazing things, so long as they have the proper supports around them, and the system has the power to provide an educational environment that is non-discriminatory, fair (equitable access to the curriculum), and filled with opportunity (find success regardless of needs).

According to the National Association of Special Education Teachers, a *learning disability* affects the brain's ability to receive, process, store, and respond to information. While a learning disability cannot be "treated," in the same sense as physical or mental health disabilities, proper supports can reduce its effects while also increasing productivity and overall happiness.

A *mental health condition* refers to psychological, biological, and behavioral factors and their impact on overall wellness. It involves thought processes, the ability to cope with daily life stressors, and actions. Mental health conditions may be treated in multiple ways, including peer support, psychotherapy, medication, alternative therapies (meditative activities, reiki, herbal remedies, light therapy, etc.), hospitalization, and brain stimulation therapies (electroconvulsive therapy, deep brain stimulation, vagus nerve stimulation, etc.).

A *physical disability* can be defined as a long-term impairment of the body that impacts one's daily functioning. Treatment of a physical disability may involve physical or occupational therapy, surgery, training, and counseling focused on how to live with the disability or an alternative path to manage living with the disability.

While these distinctions may help guide plans of action, it is important to note that multiple disabilities can exist simultaneously. This is often referred to as comorbidity. The following scenarios illustrate the importance of taking a broad, panoramic view of your child and all of their areas of need:

1. Dayna demonstrates symptoms of explosive anger disorder. Her support team treats Dayna based on these symptoms. However, while treating Dayna's mental health needs, they have failed to understand comorbidity and have therefore overlooked patterns that suggest a severe learning disability. The feelings of hopelessness and frustration brought forth by Dayna's undiagnosed learning disability have led to the onset of her mental health needs. By not addressing the root causes of Dayna's mental health challenges, the symptoms of both conditions persist.
2. Sawyer has a physical disability, as well as a mental health condition. His support team has been able to recognize and distinguish between both diagnoses. They analyze each in order to determine needs and have used this data to create a specialized treatment plan that addresses each diagnosis as its own unique entity. In time, and with proper support provided by qualified professionals, Sawyer learns to manage obstacles created by his physical disability while also making strides in his mental health needs.

Proper distinction and diagnosis between conditions are imperative. An awareness of comorbidity and understanding how potentially misleading behaviors can intertwine with actual diagnoses is necessary in order to put appropriate supports and specialized teams in place.

Does my child have a disorder or disability?

In these modern times, parents like you are constantly fed information about disabilities in children and adolescents. Whether through various media platforms, good old-fashioned marketing, or any other means, the constant flashing of neon signs and ear-buzzing chatter about the needs of our youth may make you feel as if your child surely has a need which requires immediate action. Much like searching physical ailments online and then convincing yourself you have every illness you've ever read about, it is easy to see threads of symptoms in our children and weave them together to create a diagnosis. The opposite also can happen. Parents may observe patterns that indicate a disability but then incorrectly misread those cues as being developmentally appropriate behaviors or simply "growing pains."

To help determine whether symptoms or behaviors require deeper investigation, let's look at some indicators that may suggest your child's needs stretch beyond the typical. It is important to note, however, that these indicators are not all encompassing nor are they absolute. In other words, the indicators listed are not sole evidence that a disability is present. Symptoms may manifest in ways that do not tell the full story. For example, a learning disability may actually present itself as a mental health condition. Or, behaviors that suggest a mental health condition may be the result of an undiagnosed learning disability.

In order to avoid misinterpretations or accidentally jumping to conclusions, indicators should be observed consistently, over time, and should be viewed with all other circumstances in mind. Cultural elements, language habits, family values and norms, parenting styles, background, and experiences, should all be considered.

Potential Indicators of a Learning Disability

- Delay in language development
- Difficulty and/or frustration in learning colors, shapes, sequences, letters, and numbers
- Difficulty understanding and/or relaying information with spoken word
- Difficulty following directions when attempting to do so
- Inability to focus or concentrate on non-preferred topics and/or activities for extended periods
- Inability to put thoughts on paper or into spoken word
- Hyperfocus on preferred topics and/or activities
- Challenges with spelling, handwriting, or computations
- Trouble retaining new information/poor memory
- Inability to follow multi-step directions
- Difficulty in social situations and/or trouble with social cues
- Disorganization that impacts daily life

- "Acting out" in social situations in the classroom
- Seemingly "in their own thoughts"/ distracted

Potential Indicators of a Mental Health Condition

- Extreme and/or excessive worry
- Avoidant behaviors
- Excessive distress when a change in routine occurs
- Excessive negative self-talk that impacts daily life
- Antisocial behaviors (beyond shyness and introversion)
- Physical ailments that accompany underlying worry
- Excessive and uncontrollable panic
- Extreme shift in mood
- Obsessive unwanted thoughts or repetitive behaviors that impact daily life
- Risky behaviors and/or impulsivity
- Racing thoughts or hyperactivity
- Extreme hostility or aggression
- Lack of empathy
- Depression, withdrawal, hopelessness
- Frequent sadness or loss of interest
- Loss of appetite and/or sleep disturbance

Potential Indicators of a Physical Disability

- Difficulty sustaining energy/low stamina
- Low muscle tone
- Trouble with balance
- Difficulty moving, walking, lifting, sitting up, or standing
- Squints or stands very close to an object before recognizing it
- Difficulty hearing, ignoring, or asking you to repeat yourself
- Avoidance of physical activities
- Difficulty with coordination
- Trouble with scissors, grip, buttoning, or zipping
- Difficulty manipulating toys
- Difficulty performing daily life activities

Other Possibilities to Consider

As described earlier, there are a number of symptoms that could indicate a disability. However, seeing these symptoms does not necessarily equate to a diagnosis. When reflecting on observations and indicators, consider all the potential drivers that could be causing them.

If you recognize these, or similar drivers in your child's life, work to decrease their impact. Talk to your child's pediatrician, school counselor, or other supports that could lead you to answers. Talk to your child

FIGURE 2

Potential Drivers to Consider

Social	Environmental	Medical/ Physical Health
Bullying or harassment	High-crime neighborhood	Chronic illness
Friendship issues	Refugee	Chronic pain
Grief/loss	Poor living conditions	Poor nutrition
Sense of belonging	Tumultuous home life	Unhealthy sleep habits
Social media influence	Political unrest	Poor hygiene
Excessive screen time	Societal shifts that disrupt daily life	Lack of exercise
	Natural disasters	Excessive screen time
	International crisis	Use of drugs or alcohol

directly and work with them to decrease their impact. If you still do not see significant positive changes after using interventions for a fair amount of time (roughly six to eight weeks), additional options are available.

If You Suspect a Disability or Condition...

Once all other potential factors and drivers have been eliminated, there are a number of steps you can take if you suspect your child has a learning, mental, or physical disability. A more in-depth examination of each step is outlined in later chapters:

- **Talking to school staff.** Make staff aware of your concerns, ask what they have observed and if this is typical for your child's stage of development, considering factors such as personality, energy level, culture, and so forth. Together, you and your child's school can brainstorm possibilities for data collection, information gathering, and next steps.
- **Requesting input from the school psychologist, nurse, occupational therapist, physical therapist, speech and language pathologist, resource team, or its equivalent.** While they cannot diagnose students, qualified school personnel with expertise in areas related to your specific concerns can determine if your child displays tendencies toward a disability or condition. Results of their evaluation could be used to determine eligibility for an official treatment plan.
- **Consulting with other caretakers and helpers in your child's life.** Reach out to your child's coach, tutor, camp counselors, after-school program staff, or any adult in your child's life to better understand and learn what they have observed. This multi-vantage point approach could provide you with a wealth of informal information that can be used later when discussing options with educators and qualified professionals.
- **Talking to your child's pediatrician.** Explain what you have observed, what others have observed, and listen to their clinical thoughts. Your pediatrician may provide you with scales or ratings to complete,

referrals for further guidance, or actionable steps to take in the short term.

- **Reaching out to a mental health or cognitive development professional.** A quick consult with a mental health professional could provide you with answers. If needed, an evaluation or screening by a qualified professional will provide a strong foundational understanding of what is going on, as well as recommended steps for success.
- **Inquiring about possible tests that would help rule out or pinpoint possibilities.** Lab tests, physical and medical exams, a review of your child's personal history, intellectual assessments, and mental health screenings can help in understanding the whole scope of your child's needs.
- **Doing your own research.** Join local organizations, parent groups and forums, attend workshops or parent training seminars, or simply read relevant books or peer-reviewed research journals to learn more about what you are seeing, the potential inner workings of your child, and how you can best parent them.
- **Taking note of the symptoms.** Have they lasted longer than six months? Are they consistent? Do they continue no matter what modifications to routine, environment, and support you provide? Are they appropriate based on your child's age? Do they seem to be somewhat in tune with your child's classmates and peers, or do you feel that the symptoms are on another level? These notes can be used to

help you, as well as those from whom you seek advice, in determining a plan of action.

The thought of your child suffering from a disability can feel both distressing and, if you are not sure of which direction to take, a little frightening. Still, it is important to remember that your child is not alone in their battle to overcome such challenges, nor are you alone in your battle to protect them and provide them with top-notch support.

The first step in overcoming a disability or condition is pinpointing the precise problem. From there, you can find a supportive group of peers who understand the situation, work with high-quality specialists, and provide your child with the means necessary to thrive.

Self-Diagnosis and Self-Labeling

Recently, there has been an increase in self-diagnosis among children and adolescents. Some suggest that factors, such as greater access to information about various disabilities, reduced stigma, and increased empathy towards those who require individualized support, have led to this rise.

Once considered a private matter by some, increasing awareness and normalization of diverse needs has led to a movement to embrace, protect, and appreciate these differences. This, in turn, has created a platform for young people who seek to better understand themselves, to relate with others, and to feel a sense of purpose in advocating for and educating others about diverse needs.

Some young people now consider the diagnosis and management of certain disabilities and conditions as a means to be seen and acknowledged. Some view it as a means of connection. Still, others view self-diagnosis or self-labeling as a way to excuse behaviors and avoid accountability. Clinical professionals have noted that social media and our current culture have glamorized and romanticized various diagnoses, leading to occurrences such as TikTok's "sick-role subculture."[2]

Peer connection, stress reduction, and a sense of community, based on shared experiences of symptoms, accounts for much of the surge in self-diagnosis. The rise in self-diagnosis online and in various other settings has sprouted communities focused on creating emotional outlets and relationship-building through a perceived or desired common struggle.[3]

Sheer curiosity and lack of accurate education about disabilities or conditions may also lead to self-diagnosis or self-labeling. In a recent study, five hundred TikTok videos related to mental health advice were analyzed to assess their accuracy and the potential risk of their content. Results indicated more than eighty percent of the content was misleading and fourteen percent could be potentially damaging.[4] Nevertheless, social media algorithms and trends only lead to increased exposure to this content.

If your child or teen has self-diagnosed a condition or disability, the first step to take is to simply have a good conversation with them. With compassion and an authentic desire to better understand, try to identify what led your child to feel they may have this condition. Go into the conversation with empathy and a willingness to hear...

- How or where your child heard about this condition.
- What they know about the condition.
- The potential positives of being diagnosed with this condition (attention, academic support, sense of belonging, etc.).
- Alternative answers that could account for their feelings, thoughts, and actions.

Also, it would be beneficial to educate them, as well as yourself, on the condition. Review multiple, reliable, and evidence-based sources together, ask questions, and encourage your child to ask questions, too. Next, model coping strategies that align with their symptoms. Frequently use and reflect on these strategies with them. Encourage them to explore other coping strategies and determine which work best for them. If this proves ineffective, consider seeking the help of a professional.

Misdiagnosing or Mislabeling Your Child

Any loving parent wants the best for their children. As such, they do research, they read helpful books and blogs, they chat with other parents, and they strive to provide every resource available to secure a path for their children's success. In this quest to protect and provide for their kids, however, misreading and misinformation may lead them down a path toward misdiagnoses or misunderstandings.

A few keystrokes and swipes provide access to an abundance of information on child and adolescent disorders. Not all of it is accurate or helpful. Even without seeking such information, you have probably been presented with pharmaceutical marketing that often is not based in research, contains misleading and flawed information on childhood diagnoses, alarms you with overwhelming warnings regarding children's needs, and pushes you to act by sharing terrifying outcomes if these needs are left unmet.[5]

This excessive access to information has led to misinterpretations and a devaluing of professional definitions of childhood needs, which can lead to false understandings or interpretations of a child's actions and behaviors.[6]

It is not uncommon to feel confused or overwhelmed when it comes to your child's behavioral, academic, social, or emotional decisions. The culture of modern family life can foster less tolerance for any deviation from the traits and behaviors that are expected of children.[7] This pressure to understand and find fast solutions when kids do not present themselves in ways that reflect accepted norms or the "status quo" can increase the potential for a misdiagnosis.

As a parent, when determining if a disability or condition is present, your approach must be practical and vigilant because an inaccurate diagnosis could lead to a number of adverse consequences. Namely, an improper diagnosis could cause a softening of expectations, which could lead to inadequate engagement with practical life skills, lowered motivation, and negative self-image. The danger of kids being unfairly labeled,

FIGURE 3

A Formula for Potential Misdiagnoses

The desire to understand our child's questionable decisions or actions and observable similarities to symptoms we research

+

Broadly defined diagnostic criteria of a child's needs based on an excessive amount of information available to us

+

Difficulty accepting and embracing variation due to the demanding and arduous life of today's families

+

Pressure felt to create a plan of action

=

Misdiagnoses

getting bullied, or facing other social hardships also increases.

When we misdiagnose children without professional guidance, we do more harm than good. Therefore, it is crucial that proper steps are taken if you suspect your child has a disability or disorder. This includes consulting with qualified professionals to reliably validate the situation and then designing interventions and treatments based on the whole child.

1. ADA.gov (2020, February 28). Guide to disability rights laws. U.S. Department of Justice Civil Rights Division, Americans with Disabilities Act. https://www.ada.gov/resources/disability-rights-guide/#top.
2. Yaqub, T. (2022). 77.2 Psychiatric self-diagnoses and suspected social media contagion effects: What is the role of the child and adolescent psychiatrist? *Journal of the American Academy of Child & Adolescent Psychiatry, 61*(10), S107–S108. https://doi.org/10.1016/j.jaac.2022.07.439.
3. Martin, J. (2023). Mental health and the TikTok effect. *Therapy Today, 34*(3), 18–21.
4. Ibid.
5. Tellings, A. (2020). Diagnosis pressure and false positives: Toward a non-reductionist, polytomic approach of child mental problems. *Philosophical Psychology, 33*(1), 86–101.
6. Batstra, L., & Frances, A. (2012). Diagnostic inflation: Causes and a suggested cure. *Journal of Nervous and Mental Disease, 200,* 474–479.
7. Ibid.

CHAPTER 3

Guidance, Data Collection, and Treatment Plans:

Where to Go for Information? What Are the Main Treatment Options?

If your child is showing signs of a disability or condition, gathering information is an invaluable first step. This means collecting evidence and viewing your child's behaviors with an objective mind to better understand what is going on. That way, you can get definitive answers as to what challenges your child is facing in order to appropriately support them.

When searching for and collecting evidence, ask yourself:

- *Who do I turn to for guidance?*
- *What do I ask them, and what will they ask me?*
- *What are my options if my child actually has a disability or condition that impacts their daily life?*

Seeking Guidance and Support

If you notice actions and behaviors that seem "off," or the absence of certain actions and behaviors strike you as abnormal - not reaching developmental milestones, social problems, or emotional disparities - trust your gut. Start keeping a journal of what you notice and observe. Note details about the actions and behaviors whenever possible, including the context in which they occur, the setting in which they occur, and the times they occur.

Next, research developmental milestones that should be met around your child's age. Milestones can include gross motor skills, academic and cognitive abilities, social-emotional behaviors, and communication skills. In your journal, note what milestones were met or not met. If you feel it would be beneficial, research any symptoms you are observing by visiting websites of reputable institutions, such as a children's hospital, the Centers for Disease Control and Prevention, or your state's Department of Education. It should be noted that searching for specific symptoms will most likely lead you to diagnosable conditions (as the old adage says, *Seek and you shall find*). For that reason, please take everything found in your searches with a healthy dose of caution. Your goal is to simply gain more insight into *potential explanations and/or possible remedies* for the behaviors you are noticing. In your journal, write down the key ideas or concepts you find.

Once you have collected evidence, through observations and research, reach out to your child's pediatrician. Express your concerns and share your findings. Your pediatrician may perform a developmental and/or behavioral assessment, which helps them better understand where your child is in terms of typical developmental standards, before referring you to other specialists.

You also may want to reach out to your child's school. In writing, explain your specific concerns, describe what caused you to become concerned, and request that the school perform an assessment. While some schools or districts offer assessments and screenings to determine if a physical disability is present, all schools provide assessments to determine whether an intellectual disability may be present.

Data Collection: What to Request and What to Gather

When it comes to identifying the potential presence of a disability or condition in your child, the more data you can collect, the better. The key is to gather data from a variety of settings and situations. This makes it easier to see and understand the magnitude of any potential disability or condition, as well as the drivers behind the symptoms.

Data collection can begin at home. Consider the following: How and where does your child spend their day? What do they do at home? At school? In the community? Do they ride the bus to and from school? Are they involved in aftercare or any extracurriculars? Who are the trusted adults with which they regularly interact?

Once you have a solid conceptualization of your child's day, start thinking about the people who can help you capture observational data, including the specific information you'd like them to note, and the circumstances or situations that most often cause your child's symptoms to present themselves. This is an opportunity to create a data-capture plan that can be used throughout your child's day. Ideally, you will be able to collect this data for at least a week or in increments over a period of time. If this is not possible, however, any amount of data over any length of time can still be beneficial.

Data also can be gathered from existing documentation. In fact, most specialists and evaluators will request existing records to help them develop a full and comprehensive portrait of your child (see **Figure 4** on page 35).

You can prepare a binder with this information ahead of time to help speed up the process. To start, organize your child's medical history. Medical history can include doctor's visits, hospitalizations, illnesses, evaluations (physical, mental, speech and language, etc.), medications, and any other pertinent health information. From there, add your child's developmental history, including problems at birth or in early childhood, as well as difficulties or delays with developmental milestones. Next, add academic history. Include grades, test scores, behavioral referrals, health room visits, and absence/tardy history. If needed, call the school and ask for a copy of these records. After this, add your family history, including any medical or mental health issues. Finally, include notes describing any traumatic or major life events that may have impacted your child.

FIGURE 4 ***Sample Data Collection Plan***

Data Collector/ Informal Notes Taker	Areas of Observation	Look For's
HOME: Self & Spouse Au pair	AM/PM routines (challenges with brushing, bathing, dressing), walking up and down stairs, sibling play, self-play choices, body when sitting and standing, comments from our child about energy and activity	**SOCIAL:** Withdrawal, avoidance of physical activities, non-reciprocation **EMOTIONAL:** Sadness, lack of affect, or frustration/anger when performing physical tasks
SCHOOL: Classroom Teacher Specials Teacher Recess/Lunch Aides	AM/PM routines (challenges when packing and unpacking, morning stretches), transition times, engagement in physical activities, body strength when sitting and standing, recess activity, PE engagement, energy level in comparison to peers, comfort level in group vs partner vs individual play, comments from my child regarding physical activities & energy	**PHYSICAL:** Inability to keep up with siblings and peers during active play, difficulty grasping pencils, utensils, toothbrush, scissors, etc., short spurts of energy, tiredness
EXTRA-CURRICULARS: Tennis Coach	Coordination, racquet grip, movement and agility, energy level, pace of movement/ability to keep up with the game, body strength when standing and running, comments from my child about physical activity, energy, etc.	**BEHAVIORAL:** Avoidance of physical tasks, daydreaming or distraction, finding ways to remove themselves during moments of active play

FIGURE 5

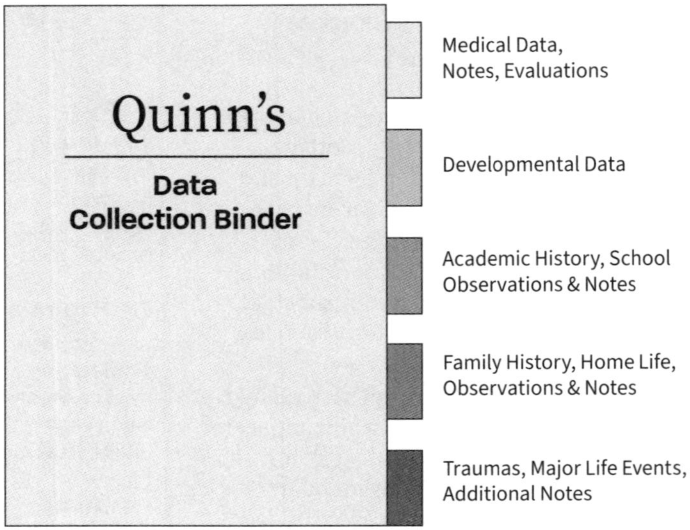

Student Plans

There are a number of options within your school and community that are meant to serve a broad range of needs. For example, a child who requires specialized medical care for a condition may receive an Individualized Health Plan (IHP), while a toddler who has been diagnosed with a disability may be supported through an Individualized Family Service Plan (IFSP).

The needs of a child who receives an IHP differ from those of a child who receives an IFSP, however, the network of school and community treatment providers are well-equipped to meet any and all needs. It is not a one-size-fits-all scenario. The remainder of this chapter focuses on Individualized Education Plans (IEPs) and 504 Plans, as these are the most common options used in school settings.

504 Plans

The Rehabilitation Act of 1973 is a law that prevents discrimination of persons with disabilities. This law applies to all federal programs and organizations within the United States. Part of this law, Section 504, states that a personalized plan, which is called a 504 Plan, can be offered to students with any disability or condition that impacts their ability to learn or that limits one or more major life activities.

Applicable major life activities are determined by a specific list of indicators. These indicators include, but are not limited to, the following:

- ✓ Thinking
- ✓ Learning
- ✓ Hearing
- ✓ Seeing
- ✓ Bending
- ✓ Reading
- ✓ Concentrating
- ✓ Standing
- ✓ Working
- ✓ Caring for Self
- ✓ Sleeping
- ✓ Lifting
- ✓ Breathing
- ✓ Eating
- ✓ Speaking
- ✓ Communicating

Accommodations written into a 504 Plan are provided in the general education setting by general education teachers. This includes all teachers and all school settings that a child encounters during their school day. A 504 Plan is a legally binding document. Although there are protections in place, the safeguards required in a 504 Plan are not as strict or as strenuous as those required in an IEP. In fact, a child who has an IEP also can be eligible for a 504 Plan. However, a child with a 504 Plan may not be eligible for an IEP.

If your child does not qualify for an IEP, but needs additional support, you may want to consider a 504 Plan. The definitions and legalities for qualifying for a 504 Plan are a bit more flexible when compared to an IEP.

IEPs

An Individualized Education Plan is put in place to provide special education, related services, such as occupational therapy, parent training, or transportation, and supplementary aids (assistive technology, adapted materials, or a one-on-one assistant) to a child who has a disability. A child is eligible for an IEP if they have been diagnosed with at least one of the thirteen disabilities designated by the Individuals with Disabilities Act (IDEA), and if their educational abilities have been affected as a result of their disability.

Modifications, supplementary aids, and related services provided to a child with an IEP may be provided in their general education setting, or in other educational settings if it is determined that the general education setting is not conducive to their success. This

FIGURE 6

Individuals with Disabilities

The Individuals with Disabilities Education Act was enacted in 1975 with the goal of assuring students with disabilities receive individualized free and appropriate public education (FAPE) in a least restrictive environment (LRE).

This means that students who have at least one of the thirteen qualifying disabilities outlined in the act are guaranteed a legally binding plan of action, called an Individualized Education Plan. An IEP includes specialized techniques that extend beyond the parameters of traditional classroom approaches. The IEP team continuously tracks progress, outlines necessary services and supports, and adjusts plans to meet targeted needs.

Qualifying Disabilities

- Intellectual disability
- Speech/language impairment
- Specific learning disorder
- Deaf or hearing impairment
- Emotional disturbance
- Other health impairments
- Autism
- Developmental delay
- Orthopedic impairments
- Visual impairments
- Deaf-blindness
- Traumatic brain injury
- Multiple disabilities

plan is legally binding. Therefore, it must be followed as written, reviewed for effectiveness, and enacted with fidelity.

Accommodations versus Modifications

Two terms you will often hear in any treatment planning meeting are *accommodations* and *modifications*. While they may sound similar, these supports differ in significant ways.

Accommodations are typically seen in 504 Plans. **An accommodation increases access to the curriculum.** It is an adaptation that can be provided within the general education setting and does not require changes to a child's learning or expectations. Examples include:

- Preferential seating
- Frequent breaks
- Directions presented orally
- Extended time to complete assignments

A modification, however, alters how a child learns, including the expectations around their learning outcomes. Examples include:

- Reduction of workload
- Alterations in curriculum or in behavioral expectations
- Alteration of grading standards

Recognizing potential signs of a disability or condition, and knowing what steps to take thereafter, can feel daunting. Knowing who to reach out to, how to gather meaningful data, and how to analyze this data is crucial in making the right decisions moving forward. Once you have ample evidence from multiple sources, you can work toward determining how to best support your child.

CHAPTER 4
Testing and Evaluation Options: Which Is Best?

As a parent, it can sometimes be difficult to know whether or not your child needs an evaluation. This decision requires you to consider...

- Whether your child is where they should be in relation to other children their age in terms of the academic, behavioral, and emotional challenges you may be observing.
- The severity of the challenges you have observed.
- Other factors that may be influencing your child's performance, as described in Chapter 2.

Once you've decided to have your child evaluated, determining which evaluation tool is most appropriate can seem even more daunting. The following list is designed to help you. It includes a summary of the most common evaluations for children. A flow chart also is included to help guide your decision-making process. In addition, suggestions on choosing the right evaluator to meet your needs and the needs of your child are provided, along with what to expect during the evaluation process, how to use the evaluation report, and what options are available if the cost of a private evaluation is unaffordable.

Evaluation Tools

Child Find

What it measures:

Any disability that may require modifications to your child's education.

How it is conducted:

This evaluation is conducted by the school team, **after** a request is made by you, the school staff, or a representative from a state agency. Once a request is made, and you have given your consent to move forward with an evaluation, the school will perform a comprehensive individual evaluation of your child. This evaluation must take place within sixty days of parental consent. After this, an IEP eligibility meeting is conducted with you and appropriate school staff or state agency employees, such as a resource teacher, classroom teacher, school psychologist, or administrator.

Typically, the school will ask you to complete a parent questionnaire that may include questions related to your child's developmental milestones, health, their strengths, areas of concern, and other topics that will assist in developing a fuller picture of your child. The school also may perform one or more focused classroom observations in order to better understand how your child performs in the school setting. All data points will be reviewed and discussed during the eligibility meeting.

Finally, a determination will then be made that either...

- A disability is present which impacts academic performance.

Or

- No disability is present and/or academic performance is not impacted.

If it is agreed upon that your child does have a qualifying disability, your consent to move forward with the creation of an IEP will be requested. You will be provided with informed consent stating what the process entails and your rights throughout the IEP process. The team then has thirty days to craft an IEP.

Next, you may either provide your signature stating that you have read and agree to the plan, or you may request an Independent Educational Evaluation if you do not agree with the determinations and steps outlined.

Reevaluations to ensure your child's needs are still being met are conducted every three years thereafter.

Independent Educational Evaluation

What it measures:

The learning differences, strengths, areas of need, and whether or not disabilities are present in one or more subject areas.

How it is conducted:

Typically, an Independent Educational Evaluation (IEE) lasts between three to four hours. An IEE can be performed either as an initial evaluation or as a reassessment if you disagreed with the outcomes of an evaluation conducted by your child's school. In the case of disputing a school evaluation, if the initial evaluation is deemed insufficient, the school may be required to pay for the subsequent IEE. If the school does not agree with your assessment that their evaluation is insufficient, you then have the right to invoke due process (see Chapter 7).

Like other evaluations, an IEE begins with the gathering of information. The evaluator may request documents, such as educational records, medical records, and state testing records. The evaluator may then perform classroom observations to get a full picture of factors that impact your child's learning. Standardized comprehensive assessments also may be administered in order to pinpoint specific areas of need.

Neuropsychological Evaluation

What it measures:

The learning styles, brain functioning, behaviors, personality, emotional wellness, and how these elements impact your child's learning. Neuropsychological evaluations may expose brain functioning strengths and weaknesses to determine if your child has specific learning needs or is twice exceptional (meaning gifted while also having a diagnosable learning disability).

Neuropsychological evaluations are comprehensive and provide a detailed snapshot of your child's overall profile. For this reason, they are often a parent's first choice for initial assessment as they can provide a strong foundational snapshot of strengths and needs. It is important to note, however, that due to their comprehensive and all-encompassing nature, these evaluations do not go too in-depth in any specific area.

How it is conducted:

A trained and licensed neuropsychologist conducts the evaluation, which usually consists of multiple-hour and multiple-day sessions (typically two- to six-hour sessions over a two- or three-day span).

A neuropsychological evaluation typically starts with the gathering of information. The evaluator will use this material to build a profile based on medical, academic, psychological, and other background documentation. They also will request an initial intake interview with you. This allows them the opportunity to get to know you and better understand your child's needs from your perspective.

Next, the evaluator will spend time with your child. They will build rapport, observe, and facilitate a battery of comprehensive standardized assessments to gather data. These assessments may gauge skills (academic, visual, language, etc.), developmental and academic levels (intellect, executive functioning, cognitive functioning, memory, etc.), and social-emotional functioning (social functioning, emotional intelligence, mental health and well-being, resiliency, coping, etc.).

Classroom observations or outreach to various supports in your child's life, such as teachers, therapists, or school counselors, also may be included in the evaluation. Once the evaluation has been concluded, the evaluator will write up an extensive report which they will share with you. During the final meeting, you will have time to review the results and scores with the evaluator, ask any lingering questions, and go over focused ideas that the evaluator has on how to best support your child academically, emotionally, and in all settings.

Psycho-educational Evaluation

What it measures:

The possible learning disabilities or mental health conditions that could impact your child's learning. Psycho-educational evaluations determine how your child thinks, as well as how they perform in academic settings. Areas such as IQ, cognitive functioning, learning style and differences, mental health, social-emotional functioning, and developmentally appropriate academic skills are focused on in order to determine the extent to which any detected conditions could be impacting your child's performance.

Psycho-educational evaluations are less comprehensive than neuropsychological evaluations. As a result, they may be the best choice for children who demonstrate specific intellectual and classroom needs, and/or children who have previously completed a neuropsychological evaluation but need a targeted follow up to track progress.

How it is conducted:

The evaluation is conducted by a school psychologist or licensed clinical psychologist. A psychoeducational evaluation usually lasts between five to eight hours over the course of one to two days.

These evaluations begin with information gathering. This includes developmental, medical, academic, and family history. The evaluator will then use this information to determine areas of focus during their time with your child. Interviews with you, your child, and/or other relevant stakeholders may be requested. Next, the evaluator performs standardized assessments with your child in order to determine their performance in relation to their peers. Outcomes are then analyzed, and a detailed report is written.

Psychological Evaluation

What it measures:

The social, emotional, and behavioral skills, inadequacies, and root causes behind these strengths and areas of need.

How it is conducted:

Performed by a licensed clinical psychologist, these evaluations vary in time. Depending on the type of evaluation, it could take anywhere from two hours to a few hours over the span of multiple days.

The evaluator will conduct a clinical interview with your child and will speak with you, too. A series of formal or informal assessments to measure mental, behavioral, personality, and/or overall cognitive functioning may follow. A social history evaluation may also be included in the process. This involves gathering information related to the impact of family, background, culture, and environment on a child's academic, emotional, and behavioral characteristics. Outcomes are analyzed before a diagnosis and treatment options are discussed.

504 Eligibility Meeting

What it measures:

Whether or not your child has a disability which significantly impacts their ability to learn.

How it is conducted:

An Eligibility Meeting begins with a collaborative discussion and review of your child's academic performance. This meeting, which can be initiated by either yourself or the school, is held to discuss concerns and possible steps to support your child, if needed. The meeting answers two questions:

1. Does your child possibly have an impairment?
2. Does the impairment impact their ability to perform one of the "major life activities" outlined in Section 504 of the Rehabilitation Act of 1973?

An official diagnosis of a mental health or physical health impairment is not necessarily needed in order for your child to be eligible for a 504 Plan. You and members of the 504 team (the 504 coordinator, classroom teacher, administrators, school nurse, if necessary, special education teacher, and any other faculty member deemed relevant to the conversation) will review the concern, share formal and informal notes and observations, review academic history and attendance, and share any applicable doctor's notes. If your child is found eligible, you will then be invited to attend a meeting to create their official 504 Plan, which will be immediately implemented once finalized.

Psychiatric Evaluation

What it measures:

The diagnosis and potential treatment options for mental health disorders.

How it is conducted:

The Psychiatric Evaluation is conducted by a qualified professional psychiatrist. Initial evaluations can take about an hour but can be extended over a longer span of time based on needs.

A comprehensive psychiatric evaluation begins with describing present behaviors and symptoms that led you to request an evaluation. Following this, the evaluator will gather background information on your child (health, educational, social, etc.) and on family history (psychiatric, relational, etc.). Relevant tests, such as physical exams, blood tests, educational assessments, and previous mental health assessments, may be collected as well.

An interview is conducted with your child and with you, either together or separately. The purpose of this interview is to better understand the situation and how pieces fit together to both impact and be impacted by biological, social, environmental, and other related factors. Following this, the evaluator will take time to answer questions and support both you and your child. They may suggest a further assessment be completed.

Occupational Therapy Evaluation

What it measures:

The complex motor skills, including fine, gross, and visual, that can impact a child's daily life, such as their ability to perform day-to-day operations related to school, play, sensory awareness, regulation, overall functioning, and self-care.

How it is conducted:

Performed by a qualified occupational therapist (OT), these evaluations usually last between two and four hours. An OT Evaluation includes a number of activities and exercises that measure sensory motor abilities and skills. Tasks involved may include handwriting, cutting, picking up objects, buttoning and unbuttoning, balancing activities, testing range of motion, and performing other day-to-day tasks.

The initial evaluation typically starts by gathering information. The evaluator may ask for your child's history (birth, health, development, etc.) to gain a foundational understanding of needs and the root causes of these needs. From there, they will most likely request a parent interview. While casual, this interview is important. The evaluator will ask questions, such as what led to your desire for an OT Evaluation, what are your goals and hopes for this evaluation, and additional questions related to your observations and areas of concern.

Depending on their setting and needs, the evaluator also may ask for input from your child's school or other pertinent outside settings. Once the evaluator feels confident in their understanding of all the background information, they will do observations and assessments by incorporating standardized assessment exercises, such as play, verbal requests, and other means of engagement.

Speech-Language Evaluation

What it measures:

A Speech-Language Evaluation measures strengths, deficits, and contributing factors in a child's ability to form and process language. This includes the mechanical formation of words, understanding of language structure, the ability to understand spoken and written language, and the ability to express oneself accordingly.

How it is conducted:

Administered by a qualified speech-language pathologist (SLP), these evaluations usually last between three and four hours. A Speech-Language Evaluation begins similarly to an OT Evaluation. The evaluator will gather relevant information, including background, birth, medical, and educational history. They also may ask you, teachers, and other adults who care for your child to fill out comprehensive deficit checklists in order to determine which tests are most aligned with both your child's clear and subtle language/communication shortcomings.

Once ample information has been gathered, the evaluator will use this information to pinpoint which battery of tests will provide the most comprehensive and necessary information for your child's specific needs.

FIGURE 7

Which Evaluation May Best Suit My Child

This graphic is not meant to determine exactly which evaluation is best for your child's situation. Instead, use this chart as a guide to help you make an informed decision about which type of evaluator/evaluation to seek out for consultation. To determine exactly which evaluation will best meet your child's needs, please consult with your child's school, pediatrician, and the evaluator(s).

FIGURE 7

Which Evaluation May Best Suit My Child

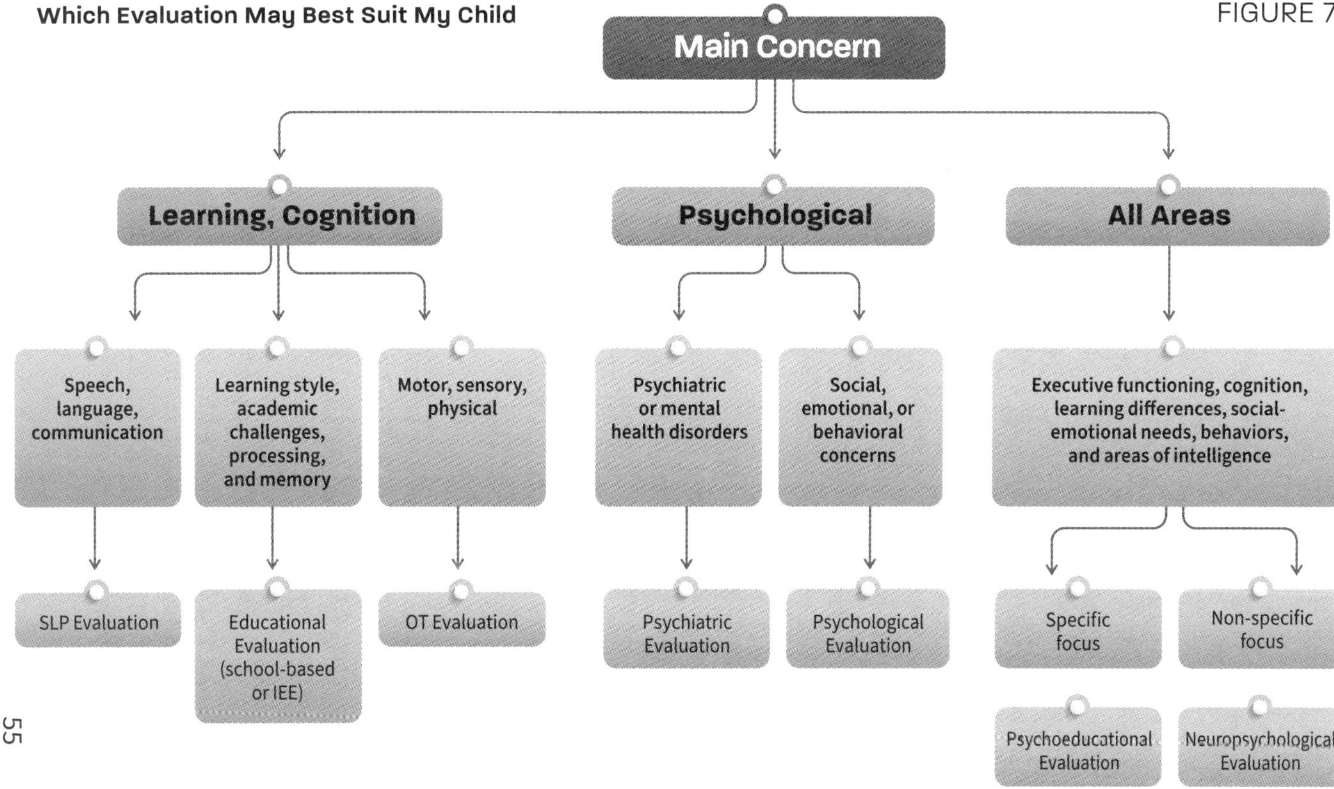

Does the Evaluator Matter?

There are several ways to find an evaluator who matches your needs. Speaking with other parents (at your school, in your district, or on local parent forums) is a wonderful way to gather evaluator referrals. Additionally, you could speak with your child's pediatrician, therapist, or other wellness provider. If you have a strong relationship with your child's school counselor, they may be able to provide you with a list of referrals based on previous parent feedback and recommendations. Some insurance companies also may provide you with a list of referrals. It is helpful to check the website of any potential evaluator and/or any online reviews.

The evaluator is arguably as important as the evaluation tool chosen. You want to ensure the evaluator has the proper education, training, experience, and qualifications before choosing to work with them. Additionally, it is helpful to choose an evaluator who...

- Has experience with children whose profiles are similar to your child.
- Has extensive experience in testing.
- Understands all relevant components related to your child's learning.
- Has a good rapport and demonstrates mutual respect for you and your child.

You have the right to forgo working with an evaluator if they do not seem like a good fit. Your gut may immediately tell you an evaluator is not right for your child, or you may need to learn more about them before making a decision. Asking questions of the evaluator and reflecting on your own instincts can be invaluable in determining how well they match with your needs.

Possible questions to ask the evaluator and to ask yourself include:

Questions for the Evaluator

1. *Tell me more about your licensure and ability to provide evaluations?*
2. *What is your experience working with students who match my child's profile?*
3. *How do you ensure cultural factors do not lead to misinterpretations or impede results?*
4. *How do you build rapport so my child will be comfortable during the process?*
5. *Do you communicate with other adults within my child's support network?*
6. *What assessments are included? What do they measure?*
7. *How do you determine a diagnosis?*
8. *What are your recommendations based on?*
9. *What is included in your final evaluation?*
10. *What is the timeline between now, the evaluation, and the final report?*

Questions for Yourself

1. *Does this evaluator communicate clearly, effectively, and with patience?*
2. *Is this evaluator willing and able to answer all my questions?*

3. *Is this evaluator willing and able to use everyday language in a manner that helps me understand the evaluation process and plan for analysis?*
4. *Does this evaluator clarify goals and educate me on factors that I may not understand because this is all unfamiliar to me?*
5. *Does this evaluator have experience working with children who match my child's age, stage of development, and challenges?*
6. *Does the evaluator use multiple modes of data collection to ensure a more accurate and whole outcome?*
7. *Does this evaluator propose reasonable time frames for assessment, analysis, and report preparation?*

School versus Private Evaluators

The decision to opt for a school evaluation over private should be based on your evaluation goals. For example, if you have a solid understanding of your child's needs and are mainly seeking school support, a school evaluation should suit your needs. A school-based evaluation also may be desirable if you would like to avoid the financial and emotional stress associated with private evaluations.

Unlike private evaluations, a school-based evaluation is free of cost. In addition, a school-based evaluation will most likely be conducted by a faculty member that your child already knows and will work with following the evaluation. This route also allows your child to remain in the comfortable and familiar setting of their current school throughout the evaluation process. Finally, the parental rights that come with a school evaluation provide peace of mind because you may seek amendments to the final evaluation report, as well as to seek additional private testing if you are unsatisfied with the evaluation report.

However, if you are not absolutely certain of your child's needs or would like support that extends beyond classroom accommodations, a private evaluation may be preferable. While licensed school psychologists or licensed evaluators can determine tendencies toward disabilities, they typically are unable to provide a formal diagnosis. In essence, a school-based evaluation can be helpful in determining plan eligibility and in formalizing a path for school-based treatment. However, the limitations of a school psychologist's scope of practice could mean that underlying conditions and needs are left unrevealed and unresolved. This could lead to further performance issues for your child down the line and could impact their ability to receive accommodations outside regular school activities (such as high-stakes testing or activities outside of school). In addition, schools are not required to comply with your request for an evaluation. Meaning, the school has the right to deny a request to evaluate if it does not believe that the data supports a need.

Private testing ensures your child will be administered standardized and evidence-based assessments by a qualified and neutral person of your choosing. Private evaluations are typically more comprehensive and involve greater attentiveness to you and your child throughout the process. Moreover, you have the benefit of exploring options and choosing a private evaluator that checks off your boxes, which in itself leads to a number of perks. You have the opportunity to ensure the evaluator chosen is trustworthy, easy to communicate with, takes the time to educate and guide you, maintains a comfortable and strong rapport with your child and yourself, provides ample relevant recommendations, and follows up with you accordingly.

Both school-based and private evaluators come with potential advantages and disadvantages. Determining which best suits your child's needs is entirely situation dependent. The charts on pages 61 and 62 can be used to help guide your decision when choosing between a school-based and private evaluator.

What to Expect During the Evaluation Process?

Evaluators recognize that the entire assessment procedure can be confusing, fast-paced, and nerve-racking. They understand you likely have little experience with the process, that you love your child, and that you are coming to them because you need answers to questions that could impact your child's life moving forward. They take this responsibility seriously and are committed to providing comprehensive and compassionate support. While evaluators may slightly differ in their approach, they generally align when it comes to the overall evaluation process.

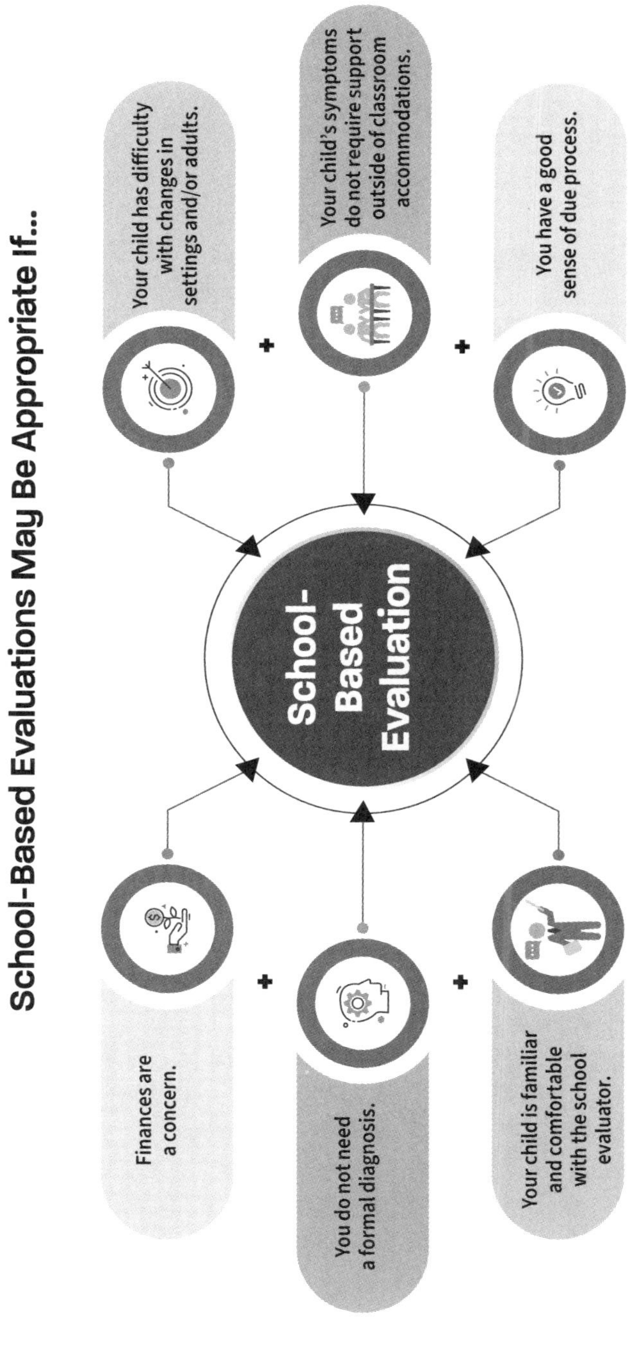
School-Based Evaluations May Be Appropriate If...
Finances are a concern.
You do not need a formal diagnosis.
Your child is familiar and comfortable with the school evaluator.
School-Based Evaluation
Your child has difficulty with changes in settings and/or adults.
Your child's symptoms do not require support outside of classroom accommodations.
You have a good sense of due process.

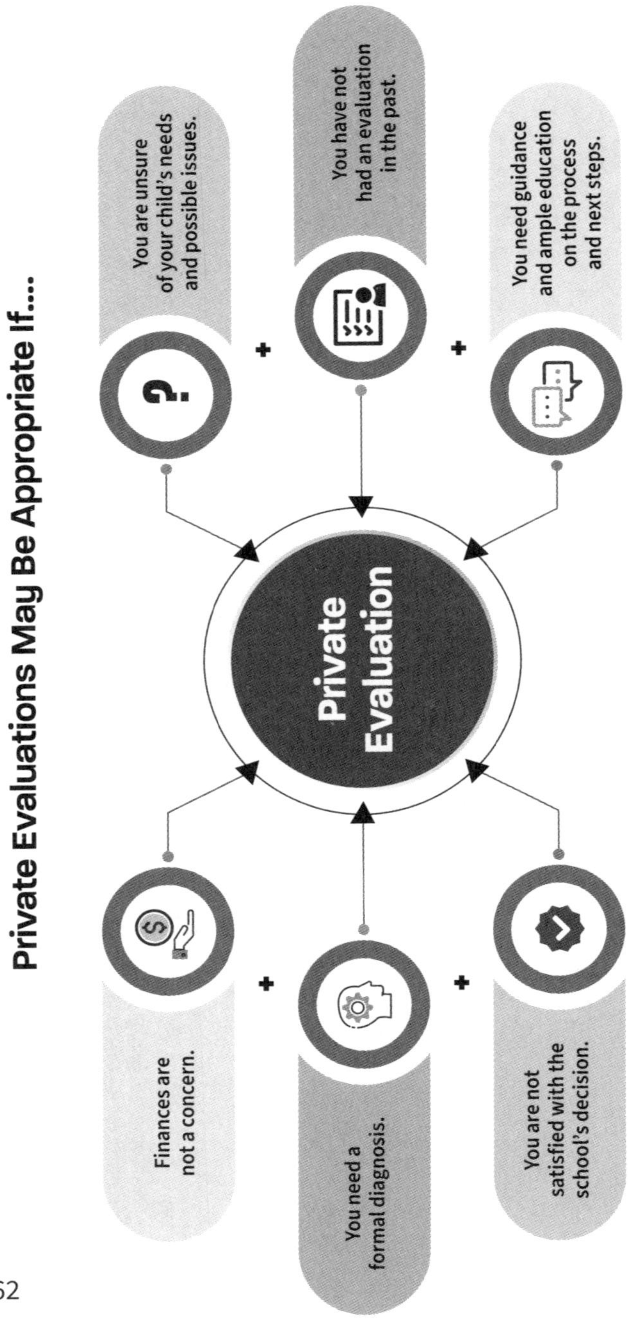
Private Evaluations May Be Appropriate If....
Private Evaluation
You are unsure of your child's needs and possible issues.
You have not had an evaluation in the past.
You need guidance and ample education on the process and next steps.
Finances are not a concern.
You need a formal diagnosis.
You are not satisfied with the school's decision.

The process begins with a parent intake meeting. During this time, the evaluator will ask questions, allow you to ask questions, and will thoroughly explain steps before, during, and after the evaluation. While you may have a great deal of information to share, you might leave out crucial points during this meeting due to the excitement and pressure you feel to convey everything in that moment. For this reason, it would be helpful to come prepared with notes that clarify the following:

- Your main concerns and where they present themselves the most.
- Overall academic, social, behavioral, and emotional performance.
- Medical history, including developmental delays or areas of note, intellectual and emotional development, major life events that may have had an impact, and problems that may have occurred during birth.

  **If your child was adopted or you do not have this history, that is okay. You can share what you know about the adoption, possible traumas, and any other pertinent information regarding your child's history and development.*
- Family history, including medical and mental health histories.
- Dynamics in the household and any elements that may be impacting your child (grief, illness, job loss, marital strife, sibling conflict, etc.).

- Observations and insights from teachers, coaches, and any other supporting adult in your child's life.
- Strengths, hobbies, interests, and any other note about what makes your child unique and wonderful.

During this initial meeting, the evaluator should thoroughly and clearly answer all your questions. The evaluator should provide suggestions for supporting your child throughout the evaluation process. For example, they may share ideas about how to...

- Prepare the day before and the day of the evaluation (proper sleep, nutrition, etc.).
- Speak to your child about the evaluation in a positive and appropriate way.
- Answer your child's questions about the process.

The evaluator may request a release of consent, allowing them to speak with your child's teachers or other supportive adults in your child's life. While not a requirement, this time spent gathering information from multiple angles could prove to be very valuable.

Also, rather than directly reaching out to those various adults, you may be given questionnaires or rating scales to complete. Like direct communication, these questionnaires and scales are meant to provide the evaluator with further data from multiple angles.

Next, the process typically involves a meeting with your child. The evaluator will use this time to build rapport, observe your child, and candidly get to know them. This will serve as a means for the evaluator to genuinely understand your child, as well as a means to familiarize your child with the evaluator. After this, the evaluation will take place.

Once the evaluation is complete and the evaluator has had time to analyze the data and write up a report, they will invite you to discuss their findings. A comprehensive report can be lengthy, as it includes information such as your child's history and their presentation, detailed results of all assessments, and suggested interventions for both home and school.

Results can be confusing, and the data may not make sense to someone who is not privy to the chosen assessments and how to read them. For this reason, the evaluator should guide you through the report, the scores, what they mean, and how the scores were determined. They also should explain findings in simple and concrete terms that are easy to understand. By the end of their explanation, you should be able to confidently summarize the findings, implications, and suggested interventions in your own words.

We Have Completed the Evaluation. What Now?

What do you do with all of this information?

A comprehensive evaluation report serves a number of purposes. Mainly, it reveals the hidden undercurrents that drive your child. The report helps you to understand what is going on within your child, how they are socially, emotionally, academically, and behaviorally impacted, areas that should be focused on in order to ensure they achieve successful outcomes, and the best approaches for meeting their needs at home and beyond. In addition, an evaluation report helps the school better understand which individualized strategies and programs could be implemented in school, by whom, and to what degree. This will ensure the school has the information it needs to provide your child with reasonable opportunities to achieve success.

How will this help me?

Some parents may find themselves struggling to understand their child. They may become overwhelmed by behaviors, gaps in academic skills, communication concerns, and other frustrations that arise from academic, behavioral, and emotional needs. They may even question their own ability to guide and connect with their child.

These fears and frustrations can be very distressing and may lead to feelings of hopelessness. The thorough results of a good evaluation, however, can provide clear-cut answers. Once you are aware of your child's needs and the breadth of those needs, you can better understand and support your child in a way that meets them where they need to be met. In fact, a good evaluation provides you with a list of resources and initial steps for getting started on this path.

More importantly, the results of a comprehensive evaluation can increase the empathy you have for your child. Rather than questioning their thoughts, behaviors, and actions, or questioning your own abilities as a parent, you will have a deeper understanding of your child and yourself. This perspective will lead to less frustration, more grace, and greater empathy.

How will this help my child?

Depending on the age of your child, you may choose to share with them the results of their evaluation in two different ways. One is in a detailed manner. The other is in a manner that simply identifies their diagnosis and explains how they can use this knowledge moving forward. There are, of course, advantages to both approaches.

If you choose the detailed route, which may be more appropriate for teens of average development, your child could use this information to increase their own self-awareness. With guidance, this could then lead to in-depth reflections on what works for them, what doesn't, and what they can advocate for to ensure they receive what they need in order to succeed in all settings. You could educate them on the options that are available to them and how and when to go about seeking these options out.

If you choose the less detailed route, which may be a better option for younger children or those whose developmental levels would indicate that this option is best, purposeful discussions regarding the results could lead to a greater sense of self and a deeper connection to others. Your child will have something concrete and common that they can grasp onto. In other words, they will know they are not an island in their thoughts, behaviors, and actions. They will know there is help available to them, and they will be able to take ownership of their diagnosis at their own discretion.

In either case, your child will feel empowered by knowing they have an identifiable diagnosis which can be overcome with a little patience and some extra work. They can feel comforted in knowing there is nothing "wrong" with them, that others have dealt with similar struggles. They will know there are ways to use their strengths to improve their areas of need, and they can use their uniqueness as a superpower once they better understand how to manage their needs.

How will this help the school?

A comprehensive evaluation report will pinpoint strengths and weaknesses and provide insights into the way your child thinks. When the school has a better understanding of behaviors, actions, and overall processing, it can use this information to zero in on evidence-based practices that best meet the needs of your child.

Additionally, the recommendations provided at the end of the evaluation report will include ideas for school accommodations. These suggestions are always taken into account and typically prove to be beneficial. In fact, they often serve as a starting point for data collection to determine next steps. This typically leads to faster inclusion of more focused and beneficial accommodations than if a treatment plan is created without the insights of an evaluation and its targeted recommendations.

What if I Cannot Afford a Private Evaluation?

Comprehensive evaluations can provide a treasure trove of information for yourself, your child, and your child's school. However, private evaluations can cost a great deal in terms of time, stress, and finances. The financial stress of a private evaluation, in particular, can prove to be a significant barrier for many families who would otherwise greatly benefit from them. Luckily, there are a number of options you can consider if cost presents a barrier.

Communicating with the school is always a good first step. As previously mentioned, school evaluations may not produce results that meet your child's needs in the most extensive way, but they may perfectly suit your child's needs depending on the desired outcomes.

If the school is unable to provide what you are looking for, the next best option is to seek support from your health insurance company. While some insurance companies will not cover testing, many will cover all or portions of testing and evaluation. If you have health insurance, contact your insurer and ask what reimbursement for testing looks like and how to maximize reimbursement.

If these initial avenues prove to be unhelpful, you can reach out to your school district's special education office, or local education-focused associations and organizations. Local government programs, clinics, and subsidies are often very helpful in determining where to find no- to low-cost evaluations.

With a bit of research, you may find local, state, or national institutions committed to supporting students with specific needs. For example, you may reach out to your local branch of the Learning Disabilities Center of America. This organization focuses on the rights of individuals with learning disabilities and can provide both advocacy and resources for low-cost evaluations.

If your main concerns revolve around mental health, the American Academy of Child and Adolescent Psychiatry (AACAP) is another nonprofit that can lead you to mental health professionals who are also licensed evaluators. If your child is 3 years old or younger, each state also has an Early Childhood Technical Assistance Center (ECTA) which can provide free evaluations for your infant or toddler.

In addition, you may find that local institutes of higher education will provide affordable evaluations through their degree programs. Oftentimes, schools that offer degrees in education, psychology, counseling and therapy, and psychiatry wish to engage their students in the experience of conducting evaluations (under strict supervision). Therefore, they are happy to provide low-cost options.

Evaluation expenses can create a barrier for children who need them the most. Luckily, there are a number of resources available to ensure your child receives a proper evaluation and subsequent resources that come from its results. It may take a bit more effort, but that effort is very much worth the outcomes that it will create for your child.

More Frequently Asked Questions

Is it too early to get my child evaluated?

You may be wondering at what age you should consider having your child evaluated if you suspect a disability. Evaluations and diagnosis can occur as young as age 2. If a disability is suspected before the age of 2, your child may be eligible for early intervention services as authorized by the Individuals with Disabilities Act. In such cases, you may seek the support of an Individualized Family Services Plan.

If a disability is suspected in your infant or toddler, do not delay in gathering information and working with qualified supportive services. Early intervention can lead to greater positive outcomes and possibly prevent more issues.

Are evaluations a "one time" thing?

Once diagnosed and provided with a treatment plan, it is recommended that your child be reevaluated every two to three years. This helps determine if your child still meets requirements for eligibility and, if so, how their needs have changed after the implementation of interventions and with their age.

Will cultural differences impact the evaluation process?

For many families, cultural elements may impact their desire to seek an evaluation. Factors, such as historical mistrust of the system, language barriers, or cultural values misaligned with evaluation and treatment, may cause families to avoid seeking this kind of support. These concerns are valid.

Misinterpretations of the results based on cultural misunderstandings or an evaluator's possible implicit bias leading to a missed or misdiagnosis, can happen. However, recent advances in the evaluation process have significantly reduced the possibility of these issues occurring.

Evaluators are now trained in cultural elements that may impact the evaluative process, their own implicit biases and attitudes, and how to neutralize these factors. For example, the current version of the Diagnostic and Statistical Manual of Mental Health Disorders (DSM-5) has dedicated a large section to what it calls "Cultural Formulation." This is a systematic procedure for successfully working through cultural elements that may impact evaluation results.

Educational Advocates Versus Special Education Lawyers

Sometimes, a little more additional help is needed. This is especially true when it comes to understanding the ins and outs of ensuring that children get what they are entitled to.

As a parent, it takes a great deal of time and guidance to understand your child's disability and needs, what services and supports are available, your rights, and the responsibilities of those who are charged with ensuring your child obtains free and appropriate education. Fortunately, educational advocates and special education lawyers specialize in helping families navigate this unfamiliar terrain.

Both educational advocates and special education lawyers aim to guide you through the special education process and remove any barriers you may face along the way. However, there are a number of important distinctions between the two. Understanding these distinctions will help you determine which is best for you and your child.

Educational Advocates

Educational advocates and consultants work to continuously stay abreast of the latest disability rights and regulations. As strong believers in the rights of all students, many of these experienced professionals have served as educators prior to becoming advocates.

When working with an educational advocate, the collaborative process typically begins with a consultation in which the advocate seeks to better understand your goals. Your child's records (academic history, communications between home and school, previous evaluations or assessments, and other pertinent data points) are then reviewed in order to determine which avenues would best suit their needs.

Advocates may then perform classroom observations to get a sense of who your child is on a typical day in their academic setting, what their classroom environment is like, and how this environment impacts them. They will have conversations with school faculty and staff, too.

Advocates will attend school meetings, communicate and negotiate with the school, and will work continuously with you and all relevant parties. Finally, they will consult with you to share their opinions and finalize next steps toward reaching goals. This may include advocating for treatment, altering current treatment plans, considering alternative educational settings, or suggesting a variety of other options to ensure your child obtains and maintains an academic framework that best sets them up for success.

When seeking the support of an advocate or a consultant, it may be helpful to ask questions, such as...

1. *Do you have any background experience in education?*
2. *What is your experience in working with students who match my child's profile?*
3. *Have you worked with my child's school or district?*
4. *If yes, what is the communication between you and the staff like (collaborative, hostile, etc.)?*
5. *What services are included?*
6. *What are your recommendations based on? How often do you perform school visits?*
7. *How do you maintain knowledge regarding current trends, rights, regulations, and laws in disability and education advocacy?*

Special Education Lawyers

Educational advocates and special education lawyers perform overlapping tasks when it comes to ensuring your child receives appropriate support. Special education lawyers serve as advocates, consultants, and liaisons between you and your child's school. However, while the primary focus of an advocate is to walk you through and support you during the special education process, a special education lawyer mainly serves as a legal consultant and representative when disputes with the school arise. Disputes may involve issues concerning evaluation outcomes, treatment plans, alternative placements, or any other special education-related issues. Unlike advocates, special education lawyers can provide you with legal advice and represent you in mediation or even in court.

When you cannot afford an IEP/Special Education Advocate or Attorney

Just as you would research available options to assist with financing your child's evaluation, similar research can be done when seeking no- to low-cost advocacy. If you are unable to afford an educational advocate or lawyer, each state and many communities have experienced professionals who are willing to help. It just takes a bit of extra effort to seek out and connect with them.

You can start by reaching out to local educational advocacy or legal aid groups for a free consultation. While you may not be able to move forward with the first group you contact, that initial call could lead to a wealth of resources and referrals to groups that may better align with your financial needs. Additionally, you may learn about organizations that provide services on a sliding scale, with payment plans, or even pro bono.

As a second option, consider checking your local government's website to learn about any state programs that provide low- to no-cost educational advocates or attorneys. Each state has protection and advocacy or civil rights offices that can provide valuable information. Additionally, you may find it helpful to reach out to various national, state, and local agencies or nonprofits that focus on disability rights. For example, reputable and strong organizations such as The Arc and PASEN (Parent Alliance for Students with Exceptional Needs) have chapters in most states. These organizations strive to provide information, advocacy, training, and other supports for individuals with disabilities and their families.

Lastly, you may find that reaching out to other parents will lead to priceless information and kindred support. You could join local parent disability-rights forums, Facebook groups, or other parent-advocacy groups. If possible, you may even want to consider starting your own parent group! You would be amazed at how many parents, just like you, are desperately seeking to share and learn from others in your area.

One important factor to consider is how you introduce or approach your child's school with your advocate or lawyer. Multiple issues, including any previous experiences the school has had with your advocate or lawyer and how your advocate or lawyer approaches the case, may influence whether or not the school will be willing to collaborate or if it will feel threatened and undermined.

Regardless, the relationship you have with the school is crucial. There are moments when you may need to play "hard ball" by drawing a line in the sand for the sake of your child, but this should be a last resort. Unless this is a necessity, you want to ensure that the representative you choose will maintain a collaborative and productive relationship with the school, will negotiate in a fair and honest manner, and will keep the focus on your child's rights and needs.

CHAPTER 5

How to Adapt to and Embrace a Diagnosis

Acknowledgement. Acceptance. Appreciation.

Learning your child does, in fact, have an official diagnosis can be quite a difficult and unsettling revelation. The realization that your child may have serious challenges to overcome, may need specialized support, and may live a life that varies from the one you had imagined can be disheartening and disorienting. However, a diagnosis should not leave you mired in sadness or confusion.

This chapter shows you how to process and accept your child's disability or condition, as well as how to shift your frame of thinking in order to better understand and appreciate your child in this new light. Research-based recommendations on how to support your child as they learn about, accept, and explore their diagnosis are highlighted, as are the effects on sibling relationships and family dynamics.

How to Process and Cope as a Parent

The finality of a professional diagnosis or proof of a condition can leave many parents feeling hopeless, guilt-ridden, incompetent, or in a state of denial. This can even be true of parents who already recognized and accepted that their child has a diagnosable condition before it was officially confirmed.

Regardless of how you feel, or your level of acceptance prior to the assessment and formal diagnosis, it can still be difficult to hear someone else share seemingly negative findings about your loved one. The feelings that come with acknowledging and accepting your child's disability or condition can be seen on a spectrum. One endpoint represents feelings like distress, disappointment, and hopelessness. The other endpoint represents feelings like gratitude, motivation, and hope. In order to lean or move closer to hopefulness, try to adopt or work toward the following mindsets:

- **See the forest for the trees.** In other words, avoid dwelling on small details and worries. Instead, focus on the big picture. Obtaining a diagnosis allows you an opportunity that other parents do not have. You now have a deeper understanding of your child's needs and how to meet them. With the overabundance of research on various disabilities and conditions, you also have access to information that can help you prepare for any possible future concerns.
- **Embrace a sense of gratitude.** A diagnosis affords you the opportunity to best support your child. You now have a name and a universally accepted piece

that completes the puzzle. Any uncertainties you had before can now be better understood, including which supports are most effective in meeting your child's needs. In addition, obtaining a formal diagnosis lessens the possibility of unseen issues negatively impacting your child down the line.

Once you have successfully shifted to a more positive, hopeful, and energized mindset, you can then work on focusing your behaviors and actions in a manner that increases your ability to process, cope, and move forward. Such positive behaviors and actions can include:

- **Welcoming your emotions and allowing them to sit with you.** You have the right to your emotions. Rather than attempting to hide or ignore them, allow yourself to feel, understand, and embrace the cycle of emotions that come with learning about your child's diagnosis. The sooner you allow yourself the time and space to do so, the easier it will be to accept your child's diagnosis and move forward with a strong sense of inner clarity.
- **Taking your time with the evaluator who provided the diagnosis.** You may feel blindsided, or you may have expected the outcomes but were not ready for the in-depth analysis. In any case, you have the right to process what the evaluator is sharing with you. Take your time. Once you have fully soaked in the main points, ask clarifying questions or any questions that come to mind. Request guidance, resources, and best practices for home and school support. Ask them to share what, in their experience, are the most effective parental strategies and

behaviors with children who match your child's profile. The more you can learn at this moment from the professional who is providing this new information to you, the sooner you will accept and embrace the diagnosis.

- **Checking in – consistently – with your feelings.** When working toward acceptance, it is imperative that you check in with yourself often and deeply. You need to understand and accept your own thoughts and needs before you can understand and accept your child's needs. Ignoring or pushing your internal signals down will only result in increased negative emotions, thoughts, and behaviors.
- **Adopting behaviors that increase parental self-confidence.** According to studies conducted by Coleman and Karraker, high parental self-confidence can lead to an increase in resilience, distress tolerance, commitment, and interest in parenting a child with special needs.[1] Healthy, positive, and appropriate behaviors include teaching discipline and holding your child accountable, maintaining appropriate expectations of your child, fostering academic achievement and ownership, providing various means for recreation and exploration, modeling and nurturing healthy emotional development, and maintaining your child's overall health.
- **Actively engaging in accepting your child's diagnosis.** Work to better understand – and help your child better understand – the disability or condition. Recognize that this one factor does not define them, and there are strategies to minimize symptoms. Acceptance includes moving forward with confi-

dence, realizing your child has a number of strengths, either because of or despite the diagnosis.

- **Prioritizing household routines and actions that will ease the impact of the diagnosis.** Take time to organize, plan, and prepare a simple and achievable set of household goals and routines that suit your child's needs. At the same time, work toward creating a calm and cohesive home environment. Together, these actions will help reduce stress and give you a strong mindset to move forward. Small goals, small steps, and making adjustments as needed will lead to a stronger understanding of, and ability to accept, your child's special needs.

Help Your Child Accept and Explore Their Diagnosis or Condition

Children and adolescents, for the most part, strive to "fit in" and want to be seen as having similar strengths and abilities as their peers. For this reason, talking to them about their diagnosis can present challenges.

Some parents attempt to avoid or downplay a diagnosis, fearing it will make their child feel "less than" or "different from" their peers. However, this avoidance or downplaying sometimes can prove harmful in the long run. Once a child reaches early to mid-elementary age, they begin to develop a keen awareness of themselves in relation to those around them. Therefore, they would greatly benefit from having ample time to...

- **Accept and familiarize themselves with their diagnosis or condition.**
- **Reflect on their personal strengths and needs, as it relates to their disability or condition.**
- **Explore strategies to lessen, or work around, their symptoms.**

Without time and freedom to explore the best options for moving forward, your child may develop flawed or unhealthy social, emotional, and behavioral coping strategies to deal with the frustration and sadness of what they think are unfixable challenges. When speaking with your child about their disability, remember to...

- **Show encouragement.** Be mindful of your tone, body language, word choice, and overall energy to ensure your child feels safe, supported, and open to learning more about their diagnosis. Use affirming language and focus on their strengths. Your conversations should be a means of building confidence and curiosity, so your child can take ownership of their disability and feel safe.
- **Set the stage for a good conversation.** Be concise and relaxed in the way you inform your child of their diagnosis. As difficult as it may be, begin by sharing the main points in a comforting and accessible way. Read your child's energy, invite thoughts or questions, and allow them to guide the rest of the conversation while you actively listen and engage appropriately. Remind them that you are always available and happy to continue the conversation

any time they have questions. Let them know you will check in with them occasionally, just in case they have concerns or questions and forget to mention them to you. Make it clear that while their diagnosis does not define them, it is a part of them that is worth talking about every so often to ensure they are getting what they need and becoming their best self.

- **Be honest and open in a developmentally appropriate way.** Share what you know, what you do not know, and offer to seek answers to any unknown questions together.
- **Acknowledge and empathize with their emotions.** Your child may initially respond with confusion, sadness, anger, lack of care, or even joy. Avoid coming into the conversation with expectations about what you think their reaction should be. Simply accept and sit with their reaction, meet them where they need to be met in the moment, and patiently continue to provide a supportive and informative safe space for them. If needed, teach them healthy emotional outlets and forms of expression.
- **Determine the best methods for dealing with peers.** Some children prefer keeping their disability private, and some want to shout it from the rooftops and educate their peers. Others prefer the "answer when asked" approach. Discuss options with your child and learn their preference. Brainstorm which approach is best depending on who they are talking to. For example, they may be willing to fully engage with a best friend about their disability while choos-

ing to minimize their conversations with peers they do not know well.

- **Maintain high standards and expect your child to do the same.** Make it explicitly clear to your child that they have one area that requires a bit more attention and focus than others, but this does not mean they are incapable of great things or that their disability defines them. Point out individuals (adults and peers in their social circle, famous people, or even popular characters from video games and media) who have similar traits and needs. Discuss how they overcome challenges, have personal strengths, and what's admirable about them.

Additional thoughts to keep in mind as you move forward:

- **Maintain an inviting space to talk.** Continue to build a safe space that allows your child to be inquisitive and reflective while growing their confidence.
- **Continuously educate yourself.** Research best practices so you can encourage and reinforce resilience and a growth mindset at home.
- **Follow your child's lead while encouraging open discussions and support.** Make time for occasional check-ins and model self-reflection, goal setting, and self-advocacy.
- **Establish routines at home.** With patience and a few "trial-and-error" runs, establish routines that align with your child's treatment plan at school. Use common language, visuals, or any other elements of the plan and apply them at home. This consis-

tency and fluidity will help with overall treatment plan success and goal achievement. It will reinforce the treatment plan's strategies and allow you to see what works, what does not work, and ways to modify the plan to best suit your child's needs.

- **Keep your child informed.** Sit with your child and discuss their treatment plan and any changes made to the plan over time. Ensure they understand their goals, any accommodations/modifications and when and how to receive them, how to self-advocate and who to advocate to, who is on their team and the supports that they can turn to, as well as how to reflect on the effectiveness of each accommodation/modification. Encourage ownership in the decision-making process of treatment planning.
- **Ask questions.** Ask how their day was through a strengths-based lens: What is one victory you had today? What is one thing you overcame today? What was one thing that made you feel good today? Learn about and praise the use of personal strengths to obtain mini victories. Acknowledge challenges in a supportive way. Express pride in their perseverance and gratitude for their grit.

Supporting the Siblings

Sometimes referred to as the "invisible child," siblings inevitably experience their own realities in the face of their sibling's diagnosis.

Studies suggest that brothers and sisters tend to have high levels of emotional distress, guilt, worry, feelings of isolation and invisibility, anxiety, and trouble with adjustment.[2] Additionally, siblings have been known to suffer from an exaggerated pressure to perform in order to compensate for their kin, feel an excessive sense of responsibility to take on household stressors, have difficulty with conflict, and suffer from psychological hardships due to taking on other family roles and self-blame.[3,4,5] In addition, family dynamics, shifts in parenting styles, and household stress levels related to caring for a child with a disability or condition can elevate these challenges.[6]

Although it is justifiable to give a considerable amount of attention and resources to a child who has recently been diagnosed, it is just as important that their siblings feel they are receiving ample affection, attention, time, and nurturing care. This can be done in a variety of ways, leading to many positive outcomes for them and your family as a whole. Ways you can support siblings include:

- **Providing connections to others who have had similar experiences.** Research suggests that siblings can greatly benefit from speaking with others.[7] Trusted social supports that exist outside of their personal situation or individuals who have endured similar experiences are excellent options for providing an outlet for letting go of negative emotions.
- **Paying attention to family dynamics.** Family dynamics play a major role in ensuring well-adjusted, content, and confident children. To the highest degree possible, try to maintain family routines, as well as high and consistent expectations for everyone. If you sense any siblings are overthink-

ing, overcompensating, or feeling unnecessary anxiety around these expectations and routines, set boundaries for their responsibilities.

- **Establishing safe, open, and accessible lines of communication.** Strong communication is essential. Talk to your children about their sibling's disability, allow them to ask questions and actively listen when they share their worries, anger, sadness, or other emotions stemming from the diagnosis. Validate their feelings, nonjudgmentally, and work with them to find healthy outlets. Remind them that their sibling is not defined by the diagnosis, and they must separate any negative feelings they have toward the diagnosis from their feelings toward their sibling. Work with them to create special signals, spaces, and supports that you can provide them in moments of need. It may be beneficial to model or role-play scenarios with them so they can practice various healthy interactions with their sibling. More importantly, don't let these conversations overtake all communication. Make a conscious effort to dedicate the majority of your conversations with them to their lives. Discuss their day, interests, needs, and how you can meet them. Demonstrate to them that they are their own individuals who deserve to be heard. Make certain they know you want special time with them, and you cherish who they are.

Allyship and Alliance as a Family Unit

Until equilibrium is found, family relationships and dynamics are often centered around the diagnosis.

This can lead to feelings of stress, dysfunction, and other unwanted emotional and relational outcomes. Siblings may feel added pressure to perform and a greater sense of responsibility to care for loved ones. Or they may experience decreases in attention and healthy attachment to their parents.

As the parent, you may feel the burden of maintaining the family unit and ensuring each family member's needs are met. The child with the diagnosis or condition may feel confusion, self-doubt, guilt, or any number of self-defeating emotions. Like many life transitions, this moment will require patience, reflection, communication, flexibility, and trial and error until harmony can be restored.

To foster and make easier the path to equilibrium and harmony, carve out dedicated family connection time. Be it weekly bonding time, daily check-ins, or any other strategy that accommodates your family's needs, use this time to reconnect and openly engage in conversations around family dynamics. As you plan these moments together, you may find it helpful to create a blueprint outlining the purpose of this family time, the energy that you hope to create, what you would like to avoid, and what would be helpful. Here is an example you can use as a guide:

FIGURE 8

Family Connections & Conversations Blueprint	
PURPOSE	■ To provide a safe, open, nonjudgmental, love-filled, and solution-focused space for honest conversations ■ To connect, bond, understand each other better, and foster cooperation and empathy ■ To focus on each other, equally, and without distraction
ENERGY	■ Safe, calm, fun, optimistic, respectful, active listening, active seeking to understand, and solutions-oriented
AVOID	■ Blame, focusing on one issue without seeking understanding or solutions, and creating a "gang up on" vibe ■ Ignoring, unfairness, or unequal attention given to each family member ■ Distractions, such as devices and avoidance topics
HELPFUL EXTRAS	■ Together, create an agenda and ground rules that focus on our purpose and hopes ■ Together, planning an activity or special treat that can be enjoyed during this time ■ Practicing how to share out, how to respond, and how to engage in difficult conversations with love and respect ■ Always end with gratitude comments, love comments, and something positive and confidence-building for all ■ Validate and acknowledge feelings

Issues you may find helpful to discuss when the topic of the disability or condition inevitably arise include:

- Thoughts about the diagnosis.
  - ▷ If and when a sibling brings up the diagnosis in conversation, approach the topic with love and curiosity. Discuss the diagnosis in a manner that gives your nondisabled child and your child who has the disability or condition the space to speak and listen. Ensure they both recognize that the disability is separate from the individual.
  - ▷ Ask each family member, including your child who has been diagnosed, what they know about the diagnosis, what they are curious about, and any worries or concerns they may have.
  - ▷ Ask each family member how the diagnosis has impacted them, or how they think it might impact them in the future, both positively and negatively. Acknowledge, validate, and work together to consider ways to avoid the negatives and increase the positives.
  - ▷ Ask each family member how they feel about the family dynamics and functioning, both positives and negatives. Work together to consider solutions to any of the negatives.
- The positives, or what each family member appreciates about the child who has the diagnosis and the

diagnosis itself (allows the child to demonstrate their ability to overcome and persevere, creates opportunities to pause and acknowledge the child's strength, provides special moments when tending to the child's needs, etc.).

In the event this conversation occurs during a planned family connection time, make certain that ground rules regarding safety, respect, empathy, and honesty without unkindness are well understood. The goal is to facilitate and guide the conversation so that it is productive and solution-focused, not hurtful and blame- or shame-filled.

1. Coleman, P. K., & Karraker, K. H. (2005). Parenting self-efficacy, competence in parenting, and possible links to young children's social and academic outcomes. In O. N. Saracho & B. Spodek (Eds.), *Contemporary perspectives of families, communities, and schools for young children* (pp. 83-106). Greenwich, Connecticut: Information Age Publishing.
2. Naylor, A., & Prescott, P. (2004). Invisible children? The need for support groups for siblings of disabled children. *British Journal of Special Education, 31*(4), 199–206. https://doi.org/10.1111/j.0952-3383.2004.00355.x.
3. Cuzzocrea, F., Larcan, R., Costa, S., & Gazzano, C. (2014). Parents' competence and social skills in siblings of disabled children. *Social Behavior and Personality, 42*(1), 45-57. doi:https://doi.org/10.2224/sbp.2014.42.1.45.
4. Naylor and Prescott, "Invisible Children?"
5. Hanvey, I., Malovic, A., & Ntontis, E. (2022). Glass children: The lived experiences of siblings of people with a disability or chronic illness. *Journal of Community & Applied Social Psychology, 32*(5), 936–948. https://doi.org/10.1002/casp.2602.
6. Cuzzocrea, et al., "Parents' Competence"; Hanvey, Malcovic, and Ntontis, "Glass Children"; Naylor and Prescott, "Invisible Children?"
7. Naylor and Prescott, "Invisible Children?"; Hanvey et al., "Glass Children."

CHAPTER 6

Before, During, and After Initial Treatment Planning Meeting

The beginning stages of treatment planning can seem like a whirlwind of voices coming from every corner, spouting confusing acronyms and seeking your input on things you may not be prepared to answer. Frankly, it can feel daunting and intimidating. While other, more experienced members of your child's team do not intend to make you feel this way, their familiarity with the process may lead them to forget that you do not have their level of understanding and comfort.

To calm the whirlwind, this chapter highlights research studies and professional experiences to help explain the beginning stages of the treatment planning process. A review of what to expect before, during, and after the initial meetings is included, as well as recommendations on how best to prepare for and optimize the experience.

Organization and Prep: Before the Meeting

Arguably the most time-consuming and challenging stage of the treatment planning process happens during the days leading up to the initial meeting. They do not, however, have to include feelings of angst or inadequacy. With a little bit of organization and preparation, you can go into the initial meeting with confidence and resolve.

Know What to Expect

Prior to the initial treatment plan meeting, expect a number of logistical and administrative measures to occur. These measures are standard procedure and are put in place to ensure a productive meeting from the start.

Your child's school will most likely contact you via email, phone, and/or text. You will receive a written notice via mail and/or text that a meeting is taking place. At least ten days prior to the initial meeting, the school will send you an invitation with the day/time of this scheduled meeting. You might also receive a parent questionnaire to complete prior to the meeting. This questionnaire will ask about concerns you have about your child, health and developmental history, any possible traumas or experiences that could have impacted your child, strengths, hobbies, and other pertinent information.

How to Optimize This Experience

If your child's case manager does not attempt to connect with you beforehand, it may be beneficial to reach out to them a few days before the meeting. Use your time with the case manager to discuss any lingering questions. For example, you may want to learn more about your state's timelines, what a typical meeting looks like at your child's school, who will attend, and what the planned agenda will be so you can add your thoughts and prepare for each step.

If you need a translator present, be sure to request this before the meeting. The school has the resources available to ensure both written and oral communications are presented in the language with which you are most comfortable using.

Take this time before the meeting to collect data, evidence, and your own thoughts about what your child needs and how the school can help. Data and evidence may include academic history, evidence related to developmental milestones, photos, observational notes, doctor's notes, or any other useful record. You may find it most effective and seamless in the long term to use a binder, file folder, e-portfolio with scanned documentation, or another organizational tool that can be continuously added to over time. Start by including documentation and evidence according to age. This will allow for an easy glance of progress over time. If possible, you also may choose to organize materials by subject matter. Some examples include:

- Academics, mental health, physical health, or behavioral presentation
- Math computation, reading, handwriting, and speech
- Doctor notes by date, teacher communications by grade, observational notes by age

Whichever method you choose, be sure to organize your reference tool in a way that best suits your style. Also, if possible, create a backup copy.

Finally, consider organizing your thoughts and exploring possibilities. Sit in a comfortable space where you can focus solely on the topic of your child. In your mind, what is it that your child needs? What barriers are preventing them from receiving or obtaining this? In an ideal world, what specifically can the school do to break or remove these barriers? If these barriers were broken, what would your child be able to achieve that they currently are struggling with?

Jot your thoughts down. If appropriate, based on your child's development and level of understanding, explain to your child that you are going to meet with helpful folks at the school to talk about how they can be of assistance. Ask your child to share their thoughts about what teachers do that is helpful for them, what makes them feel distressed or confused, and what they want the helpful folks to know in general.

If time permits, reach out to professionals, local parent information centers, state nonprofit special education advocacy organizations, parent or special education-focused forums, or search online for sample modifications and accommodations that align with your preferences and offer them as potential options during the meeting.

For additional pre-meeting reminders and suggestions, see **Figure 9**.

FIGURE 9

HAVE I RECEIVED...

- Prior written notice that the meeting will take place (at least ten days in advance)?
- A copy of procedural safeguards?
- For review, any evaluations of my child that were completed by the school?
- Consent to bring another party in with me, if applicable (advocate, lawyer, or other professional)?

HAVE I CREATED...

- A list of thoughts and questions I want to be sure are brought up during the meeting?
- A compilation of my own notes, observations, concerns, strengths, personal "get to know my child" facts, and ideas about what could possibly support them?

HAVE I TAKEN THE TIME TO...

- Ensure I am emotionally and mentally prepared for this meeting?
- Put together a meeting kit, including a notebook to record notes during this meeting and any upcoming meetings, observational notes by me and others, and any outside data that I deem useful to the team?
- Complete the parent questionnaire and/or any paperwork sent to me from the team?

Maintaining Rhythm During the Meeting

What to Expect

The pre-meeting time frame is ideal for preparation, organization, and connecting with other team members to plant the seeds of a strong collaborative partnership. Once these necessary pre-meeting pieces are in place, you can be certain that the meeting itself will be effective and productive. However, there are a few components of a treatment plan meeting that are worth noting. Being aware of the components can ease your anxiety and confusion during meeting time.

The meeting should begin with formal introductions. Everyone at the table will share their name and role (including you). This signals the start of the meeting and provides you with an understanding of who is in attendance, the nature of their relationship with your child, and what they can bring to the conversation. Next, your child's case manager or a member of the school resource team will share the purpose and goals of the meeting.

Depending on the type of meeting and the typical meeting structure at your child's school, the focus will either turn to you as the parent or walk you through the components of the treatment plan. If the focus shifts to you, the team may ask you to share your concerns, observations, your child's strengths and areas for growth, hobbies, and any other helpful information that will allow the team to better understand who your child is in and outside the academic setting. This is a good time to pull out your pre-meeting preparation notes. (If you did not prepare notes, that is okay.) There is no wrong answer, and you can always clarify or add thoughts later. If the focus goes straight into the treatment plan, take out (or request one if it has not been provided) your copy of a draft or blank treatment plan so you can follow along. Note important information and discussion highlights (and, if possible, who said them) on your treatment plan draft or in your notebook. If your spouse or partner attends the meeting with you, ask them to take notes so you can be fully engaged and present at all times.

The meeting will center around the main components outlined in the plan and should include ample discussion and brainstorming sessions. This helps ensure everyone is in agreement, any disagreements are worked out, and decisions are based on your child and their specific areas of need.

If your child is obtaining an IEP, the components to be discussed include:

- **Your child's present level of performance.** This can include observations, scores, and other data points that help paint a picture of where your child currently stands in terms of academic and functional performance.
- **An explanation of your child's annual goals.** This includes a description of individualized and explicit goals that have been created to address your child's specific needs and how progress and growth will be measured. An explanation of goals also involves what the goal/behavior or skill will look like, and the expected ratio or percentage of time the behavior or skill is expected to be demonstrated. The goal statement ends with a time frame for when the goal

should be met, where it should be met, and how it will be measured.

- **Benchmarks.** Benchmarks are measurable short-term goals that allow the team to track progress toward meeting a goal.
- **Related Services.** There are a number of related services used within the school setting to assist your child with their unique needs. Such services may include mental health supports, general health supports, speech and language supports, occupational therapy, and transportation services.
- **Supplementary aids.** Like related services, supplementary aids are meant to assist your child in accessing the same academic and nonacademic opportunities as their nondisabled peers. These aids may include one-on-one adult support or another method of receiving adult support, as well as non-person aids, such as large print text, assistive technology, braille, bumpy paper, etc.
- **Services, accommodations, and modifications in the school setting, including duration, frequency, and location of services.** This conversation will explore how long, how often, by whom, and where your child will receive all accommodations and modifications. This encompasses the classroom and non-classroom settings (field trips, lunchroom, hallways, playground/gym, transportation methods, etc.).
- **Participation, services, accommodations, and modifications in statewide assessments.** Much like the previous bullet point, this conversation covers

services provided if and when your child is engaged in statewide assessments.

- **Inclusive classroom time.** To the maximum extent possible, your child should be learning in the general classroom setting and should be engaging with nondisabled peers in all school settings. An inclusive classroom ensures students with special needs work alongside their nondisabled peers as often as possible. Usually, an inclusive classroom contains a general education teacher, a special education teacher, and/or aids who collaborate to meet all student needs. Therefore, this portion of the IEP conversation focuses on how much time your child will be learning alongside their nondisabled peers, as well as what supports will be available to them during this time.
- **Transition plans.** Starting at age 16, IEP meetings will include a discussion about your child's postgraduation goals and how to reach them. A transition plan is meant to ease their progression into adulthood by providing them with the necessary supports.
- **Extended school year (ESY) services.** Some students need support beyond the school year to ensure any gains made are not lost. In this case, ESY is a necessary addition to the IEP. ESY provides your child with supplementary aids and related services during breaks from the school year.
- **Evaluation and monitoring progress toward annual goals.** The team will discuss trends and data around the progress being made toward your child's annual goals and if this progress is adequate based

on your child's needs and the support they are being provided.

- **Parental consent.** At the end of the meeting, you will be asked to sign an attendance sheet stating you were present at the meeting and a parental consent stating you agree to the plan. It would be a good idea to hold off signing the consent form (but do sign the attendance form) until you have a few days to process the plan in a more relaxed way and in a more relaxed setting.

If your child is obtaining a 504 Plan, the components that will be discussed include:

- **Signing of Informed Consent.** Before the meeting can take place, the school will need you to sign a consent form allowing the team to evaluate your child for eligibility. Once you have done so, the meeting will officially take place.
- **Parent and/or school staff concerns.** This portion of the conversation may be guided by the parent questionnaire, or it may be a more informal and open-ended discussion about concerns and the reasons for those concerns.
- **Eligibility.** The team will guide the initial evaluation meeting using an eligibility form and asking questions. If the team agrees your child is eligible for a 504 Plan, based on the criteria outlined on the eligibility form, the meeting will transition from focusing on evaluation to focusing on eligibility. The team then has three options: your child is eligible for a 504 Plan and accommodations should be provided at this time; your child is eligible for a 504

Plan but accommodations are not needed at this time; or, your child is not eligible for a 504 Plan.

- **504 Plan development.** Plan development occurs as part of the initial evaluation and eligibility meeting, if time permits or within the next thirty days. The team will review the official 504 Plan document and work together to determine which accommodations will be included, where they will be included throughout the school day, and the person(s) responsible for ensuring access to the accommodations. Please note, however, the only accommodations that will be considered are those absolutely needed to offset the impact of your child's disability/condition on designated major life activities.
- **Parental consent.** At the end of the meeting, you will be asked to sign the plan to acknowledge that you agree to it. It would be a good idea to hold off on signing until you have had a few days to review, away from the fast-paced meeting setting.
- **Procedural safeguards.** The school must provide you with a copy of the procedural safeguards. You should review the safeguards and ask clarifying questions to fully understand your rights.

How to Optimize This Experience

Parents often express feeling intimidated or overwhelmed from the moment they step into the meeting room until they step out. The reasons vary and involve everything from the meeting room setting to the sheer number of team members present.

Treatment planning meetings typically occur in a school conference room. The room usually has a large boardroom table where everyone is seated. For some parents, this setting feels intimidating and unwelcoming because they are on the school's "home turf," trying to find space, literally and figuratively, at the table. In addition, sometimes any number of unexpected stakeholders also attend the initial treatment planning meeting. Such stakeholders may include a member of the school administration, the school counselor, the school psychologist, a county social worker or pupil personnel worker, a classroom teacher, a special education teacher, the school nurse, a county occupational therapist or physical therapist, the school speech and language pathologist, a representative from the district's office of special education, a county advocate, a translator, and other individuals who are deemed necessary when determining what is best for your child. It is important to remember, however, that each and every participant in the meeting is there for one reason – to ensure your child is receiving proper support and care.

While the visual of these professionals sitting together for the purpose of discussing your child may feel scary, their purpose for being there should outweigh any feelings of intimidation. Just like you, they are there to share what they know about their specialty, listen to all their team members, and brainstorm what steps should occur next. If you can, shift any feelings of intimidation to ones of enthusiasm because your child is going to be supported by a broad range of professional expertise.

Remember, too, that you are a key team member and not just a sideline spectator. Like any rookie entering a new situation, you may have a bit of a learning curve. The experienced team members understand this and will be happy to support you, but they will need to know what confuses you or what is new to you. So don't be afraid to ask them to pause if they are moving too quickly. Always ask questions when you need clarification or need a definition. This is your opportunity to build your knowledge of the process. One way you can ensure clear communication and understanding is to summarize and repeat back to team members what you heard them say. This will correct any misunderstandings. Be both an active participant and an active learner.

Another important fact you should not forget is that you bring expertise too – about your child. Each member of the team is coming in with their own skill set and knowledge they hope will assist in determining what is best. The general education teacher is an expert in curriculum content and classroom culture. The school psychologist is an expert in evaluation analysis and mental health resources. The occupational therapist is an expert in movement and coordination. And you are an expert when it comes to your child's disability or condition.

While other team members may have some familiarity with your child and have a surface-level understanding of the diagnosis, they are counting on you to share, interject, and educate them at this meeting. It is critical that you view and conduct yourself like an expert by explaining who your child is outside of the classroom and beyond any profile described on a piece of paper. Share what you have learned about your child's disability or condition and its impact. Also, if you feel specific accommodations may be needed, mention them. If you think certain accommodations under consideration will not be useful, explain why and brainstorm alternatives with the team. Speak up when needed, correct others when needed, and push back when needed. Healthy discomfort during discussions is expected and welcomed as you all work to create a quality treatment plan.

Lastly, slow down. Many schools have set days built in for treatment planning meetings and must stick to a strict time limit. As a result, initial meetings and some of the more engaging meetings that follow may become rushed as the allocated time frame reaches its end. If you feel this is occurring and are uncomfortable with the pace, request a time out or recess. While this may result in the need for a follow-up meeting to finish up, it will ensure the plan is not hastily created, that you are not pressured into agreeing to things you may not fully understand, and the team is focused more on the collaborative process and quality work than on the clock.

The following chart (**Figure 10**) provides a snapshot synopsis of other essential reminders and recommendations to consider during the meeting process.

FIGURE 10

HAVE I RECEIVED...

- A copy and thorough review of assessments, reports, observations, and other important documents?
- A list of those who will be in attendance?
- A copy of my child's treatment plan, or a blank plan to follow while we talk through it?
- Information regarding extended school year (ESY), transition services, state assessments, and transportation (IEP plans, only and as needed)?
- A finalized copy of my child's treatment plan at the end of the meeting, as well as ample opportunity to review it?
- Access to a qualified interpreter, if language could be a potential barrier in the collaborative process?

HAVE I REMEMBERED TO...

- Actively listen, allow myself time to process what I am receiving, and slow down before responding?
- Take notes of everything – from those who were in attendance to discussion points and data to final thoughts?
- Be aware of how I speak (word choices) so I don't put other teammates in defense mode or create harmful friction?
- Stay focused on the main points and remain concise and clear in my responses?
- Make sure I know who will be in charge of ensuring the plan is being followed, who will be involved, and how progress data will be recorded?
- Obtain the email addresses of all team members so I may send a follow-up email after the meeting?
- Take note of roles, who's responsible for what, and when it's to be completed?

DO I FEEL SATISFIED THAT...

- I had the opportunity to completely discuss my child, my expectations, and my thoughts?
- All my questions and concerns were answered fully and in a comprehensible manner?
- The team considered all facets of my child when creating the accommodations?
- The accommodations suit my child's needs to the fullest extent?
- The plan is clear enough that all staff in all settings can and will honor it?
- The process was collaborative, and everyone is on the same page?
- Those involved in supporting my child will be accountable and fully understand their responsibilities?
- The other team members offered me resources and training recommendations to help me grow as a member of this team?

Maintaining Momentum: After the Meeting

What to Expect

You had a successful team meeting – woo-hoo! Take a moment to soak in the satisfaction and relief of knowing your efforts have ensured your child will receive the support they deserve. Once you have had a chance to exhale and relax, the next step is tying up any loose ends and polishing the final pieces of the process.

Sometimes parents think or feel the meeting itself signals the process is completed. In fact, there are a few more steps that must be taken to ensure accountability, clear communication, goal agreement, and continued collaboration.

To start, be certain to send a group email to school-based members of your child's treatment team. This email should include:

- Communicating your appreciation for their time and efforts to support your child
- Recapping what was determined in the meeting
- Restating individual responsibilities and time frames
- Confirming data collection and progress tracking plans
- Inquiring when you should expect a copy of the plan if you have not yet received one
- Asking about any resources that can help you implement strategies at home
- Planning for follow-ups

Your communication to them, coupled with their responses, help ensure everyone is on the same page, and you have their agreement in written form. Create a file to save this email and any other correspondence between you and the school.

Next, take time to speak with your child about the treatment plan (see Chapter 5). During this conversation, explain...

- How the plan, coupled with hard work and dedication, will help them find success and satisfaction in school.
- The accommodations and/or modifications available to them. Use concrete examples, ask them to

share examples, and ask them to paraphrase your words to ensure they understand each service or support.

- How they can ask for their accommodations and/or modifications throughout the school day. Role-play how to request these services and supports, as well as who to ask in each school setting.

If it feels right, you may want to take this time to address how your child can reflect on whether or not a service or support works well for them. Also, get your child thinking about what alterations or changes could be made if a service or support is not working. This conversation, however, can happen after implementation of the plan. The important thing is to frequently check in with your child to ensure they are receiving their accommodations and modifications, and they are actively reflecting on the effectiveness of the services and supports.

Remember, too, you can always request another meeting before the plan's next review date if changes need to be made.

Recommendations to Optimize the Post-Meeting Experience

After the meeting, you may find yourself replaying specific comments and moments in your head. You may question yourself or the thoughts of others, wondering what could have been done better and wishing you could go back in time. Rather than reflecting with regret, adopt a mindset that is more solutions- and forward-focused.

Just as you did during pre-meeting preparation, take a moment to sit in a comfortable space where you can focus solely on post-meeting reflection. Jot down your thoughts about the following:

- *What went well?*
- *What could have gone better?*
- *Were there any moments that felt too hasty or confusing?*
- *Are there any personalities or communication styles on the team that I need to be extra aware of to ensure differences do not impede the process?*
- *Did I remain emotionally neutral and objective? If not, what can I do to manage this?*
- *Were there any individuals/resources who could have been helpful in the process but were not present at the meeting?*
- *In what areas could I have engaged more? What was holding me back?*
- *In what areas do I need more education? Where can I turn for resources?*
- *What workshops or trainings can I attend to assist in my growth as a team member and advocate?*
- *What tools or preparations will help me in the next meeting (taking notes by typing on a personal device rather than handwriting, coffee or hard candies to occupy my hands and engage my senses for better focus, taking standing*

breaks to collect thoughts, bringing a sweater if the meeting space is chilly, etc.)?

Now that you have a clearer analysis of the meeting itself, consider how you can use this information moving forward. What can you do to better prepare for the next meeting? What resources and supports do you have in the meantime? Keep in mind that this was your first treatment planning meeting. Many more will follow, and you will have opportunities for growth during each one. For now, feel proud of the work you have done and the positive impact it will have on your child.

IEP & 504 Plan Timelines

** Time frames may vary according to state and district regulations*

IEP Timeline

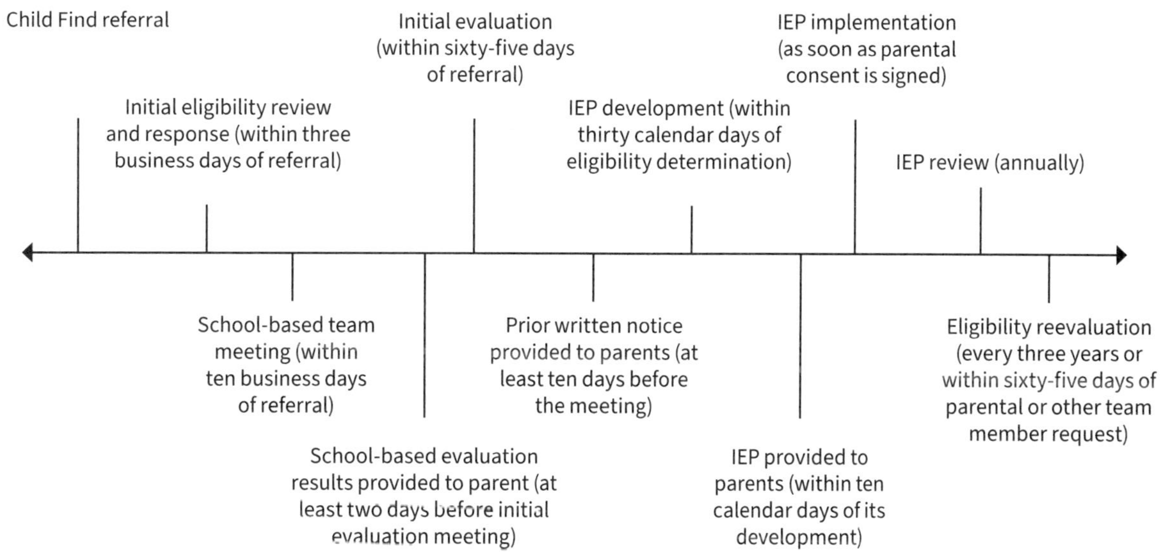

504 Timeline

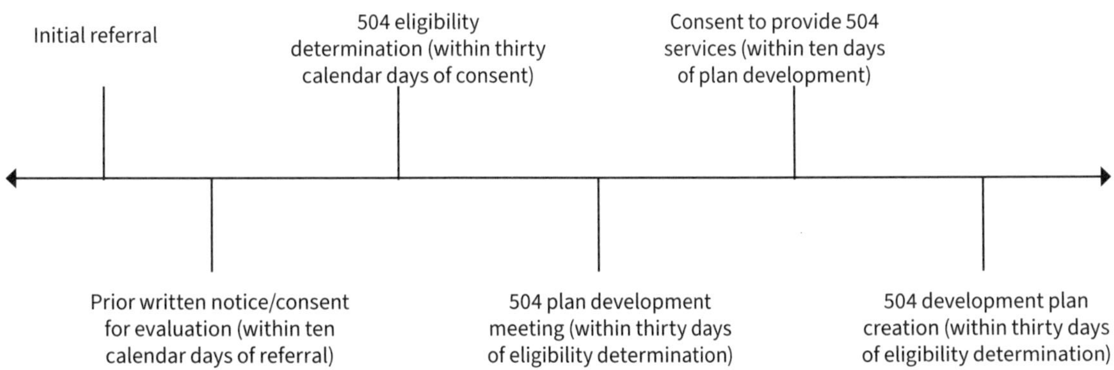

*Unlike IEP regulations, the 504 process does not include strict guidelines around parent participation or time frames. For the most accurate picture of 504 practices within your district, contact your child's school.

CHAPTER 7

Fostering and Maintaining the Treatment Dream Team: Effective Partnerships and Ensuring FAPE

(Free Appropriate Public Education)

The impact of a treatment team cannot be understated. As a united front, they have the remarkable ability to create a blueprint for your child's path to success and achievement. If the team is disjointed or flustered, however, decisions could potentially prolong or obstruct that path toward success.

A strong treatment team has high levels of mutual respect, trust, and accountability. Also, team members feel both safe and obligated to engage in conversations that may involve disagreements or discomfort in order to develop a quality treatment plan. In addition, the team engages in consistent and clear communication regarding your child's present levels of performance and any necessary adjustments to raise performance levels. A strong treatment team also ensures the home-to-school connection remains intact. An ineffective treatment team, on the other hand, shows little-to-no accountability or collaborative effort, leaving its members feeling confused, exhausted, and unsympathetic.

In this chapter, common barriers to effective treatment team partnerships are identified, as well as possible solutions and methods for creating bridges to effective partnerships. Cultural differences also are explored, as well as the steps you can take if your child is not receiving necessary supports and appropriate access or attaining equitable outcomes.

Common Barriers to Effective Partnerships

Parent Perceptions

A growing understanding of diverse educational needs has led to extensive research on both the barriers and bridges to fostering effective partnerships in the treatment planning process. From this research, a set of common themes has emerged. While there are still major strides to be taken to enhance and improve the treatment planning process on a national level, awareness of these themes can help in the context of your child and their school setting.

Common barriers expressed by parents include:

- Issues related to communication and the collaborative process

- Feelings of inadequacy or othering
- Feeling excluded or overlooked
- Rigid hierarchies in the team related to role, experience, and knowledge of the system
- General mistrust

A deeper look at parents who participated in focused research studies related to communication and the collaborative process revealed several issues that can lead to dysfunctional team energy. They include...

- A lack of quality communication in general.[1]
- Poor organization.[2]
- A sense of feeling rushed through the collaborative process.[3]

Across the board, research suggests problems arise when professionals put little effort into promoting the collaborative process in a way that matches parent needs. Studies also suggest that feelings of inadequacy or "othering" (ostracized or rejected) arise when parents feel they are being judged or blamed for the needs of their child.

Parents report they feel judged as uncaring or "bad," or feel blamed for their child's challenges by others on the treatment team.[4,5] In addition, differences related to demographics or socioeconomic status also lead to feeling inadequate or "othered" within the treatment team.[6,7,8] Moreover, parents have reported feeling excluded or overlooked when they express their hopes and goals.[9,10]

In many cases, parents felt the school-based team members dominated the decision-making process and ignored their input and reports.[11] In terms of hierarchies within the team, studies revealed parents felt disregarded and discouraged when the team used professional language and acronyms that essentially pushed them out of the conversation and disrupted the balance of power.[12,13,14]

While parents expressed distrust in general when faced with a negative treatment planning process, trust issues were particularly high around communication, collaboration, and hierarchies/imbalances of power. These issues seem to be common characteristics of ineffective treatment teams. Fortunately, there are solutions if you find yourself in a similar situation or are feeing discouraged and ignored. (For a quick reference of action steps you can take, see *Tips for a Tiptop Treatment Team* on pages 128-129.

Addressing Common Barriers

By and large, a majority of parents who participated in research studies related to treatment services reported being satisfied with the process. So, there is a high probability that you will be satisfied with your treatment planning experience, too. Still, here are a few suggestions that can ensure your treatment team is effective and, when problems arise, is open and agreeable to making adjustments.

To address issues in communication and the collaborative process:

- **Request check-ins with the team.** This can be done at the end of each meeting, at the start of each meeting, or anytime that best suits the team. Use check-ins to bring to light any disconnects that may be occurring in the collaborative process. Be direct and authentic in your concerns, and expect the same from the other team members.
- **Be the timekeeper.** If your meeting starts late for reasons that are outside of your control, remind the team you have a set amount of time available. If your time frame cannot be met, request another meeting to avoid feeling rushed or dismissed.
- **Create a plan.** Collaborate with the team prior to a meeting to create an agenda, discuss what documentation is needed for the meeting, and delegate who will bring what.

To address feelings of inadequacy or othering:

- **Proactively connect with the team.** Get to know team members and allow them to get to know you. Allow them to see your strengths, your child's strengths, and your family's strengths as a support system.
- **Address problematic comments directly.** If a team member says something that communicates judgment or blame, seek them out and privately speak with them. Use an assertive but soft tone when

explaining what was said, why it hurt, and what you expect from them in the future.

To address feeling excluded or overlooked:

- **Understand the root causes and take informed action.** Try to understand why you are being overlooked or excluded. Is it due to the meeting's fast pace? Is it due to a lack of awareness by team members that you have not been given opportunities to contribute. Is it because team members purposefully tune out or bypass hearing from you? Once you understand what is going on, address it with the team and seek a resolution that allows you to move forward together.
- **Make sure your voice is heard.** Speak up. Use a professional, but assertive tone. Look team members in the eye, speak with confidence, and command attention with your nonverbal cues.

To address rigid hierarchies or power imbalances within the team related to role, experience, and knowledge of the system:

- **Insist that "lingo" and acronyms be explained or altered for those outside of the system.** It is not difficult to alter words or take a moment to translate professional lingo into more clear and understandable terms. Treatment providers should be more than willing to accommodate these needs if asked.

To address issues of mistrust:

- **Connect with your fellow team members.** While respecting their time, try to consistently connect with team members in small ways. Check in on progress, ask how you can help, etc.
- **Work together to create a more cohesive and well-aligned unit.** Disjointed teams can lead to frustrations and mistrust. To avoid this, take a few minutes to address any areas for improvement after each meeting. Reflect on what went well and what could be better in future meetings. Working toward continuous improvement can increase trust over time, so long as team members make a deliberate effort to improve the team.

No matter where you are in the treatment planning process, it is never too late to address lingering issues. By advocating for yourself and working toward continuous improvement in collaboration, you also encourage optimal support for your child.

Cultural Responsiveness within the Treatment Team

Challenges Related to Cultural and Linguistic Diversity

Studies show that culturally and linguistically diverse (CLD) families are more likely to face challenges that extend beyond the previously described issues. These additional challenges are mainly the result of a sweeping lack of cultural responsiveness or the acceptance and inclusion of relevant cultural elements within the treatment team.

Based on accounts shared by participants, the lack of cultural responsiveness revealed itself in a number of ways:

- Lack of respect for CLD parents
- Lack of opportunity for CLD parents to advocate for their child
- An unwillingness to inform CLD parents about the educational system and the treatment planning process in general
- An unwillingness to break down language barriers to help parents through the process.

Due to these challenges, parents report feeling hurt and frustrated when attempting to collaborate with their child's treatment providers.[14]

We know most parents have a strong desire to participate in the treatment planning process, to be educated on their child's needs, and to learn about resources available to help them advocate and support their child to the highest degree. Despite this motivation and drive, sometimes these desires go unmet.[15,16,17,18,19]

Moreover, language barriers can increase treatment planning complications and decrease CLD parents' access to information.[20,21,22,23] Limited access to qualified interpreters, as well as CLD parent embarrassment at needing an interpreter, can intensify complications.[24,25] When asked directly, parents want treatment providers to reflect on and recognize their own personal biases and assumptions, and then respect and recognize differences in the traditions and values of others.[26]

CLD parents have identified a lack of cultural responsiveness and relatability as key factors that reduce collaboration and amplify mistrust. They feel disrespected, disempowered, and unheard when these issues exist within the treatment team. These feelings can then lead to even more challenges to collaboration that may be very hard to overcome.[27,28]

Addressing These Challenges

When a disconnect exists between you and the treatment team due to a lack of cultural competence or understanding, it needs to be addressed. While the responsibility of creating a welcoming, safe, and accommodating space for you and your family should primarily fall on the treatment providers and school, you must be able to advocate for yourself before you can confidently advocate for your child.

Advocating for yourself may make you feel uncomfortable or like you are showing disrespect to the team and the school, but you have the right to speak up and secure what is needed for an effective partnership. An effective partnership includes:

- **Quality language interpretation, both verbal and written.** You are entitled to clear and qualified language interpretation. Schools have resources, such as oral interpreters for meetings, language line/

phone interpreters for phone-based conversations, and translators for written words. If you are not provided with high-quality language interpretation tools, request that these resources be available or adjusted to better suit your needs.

- **Recognition and appropriate responsiveness to your cultural values and beliefs.** Cultural differences in communication styles, interpretations of respect, and other elements that affect the collaborative process must be addressed. If your team members are not educated on or do not seem to adjust their behaviors based on your social cues, educate them. Explain what you need from them and what they can expect from you in terms of communication. Have a conversation about the possible roadblocks these differences may cause and how best to avoid them.
- **Mutual respect and engagement.** When more experienced team members get into a flow, they may forget to pause and ensure you are keeping up. It is in moments like this when you can feel lost, frustrated, and disregarded. When this happens, stop the conversation. Falling behind may happen once, or it may happen multiple times throughout the meeting. Regardless, stop the conversation in its tracks. Ask the team to back up and explain what was just said. If you have input or additional questions, state them. Do not settle for anything less than mutual engagement and decision-making.
- **Request and follow up on requests to increase your knowledge.** Do not feel embarrassed to request resources (training, literature, community connec-

tions, etc.) to help you learn more about your child's needs, your rights, and the treatment process. Ask questions during the meeting, request resources at the conclusion of the meeting, and send a follow-up email asking for resources designed for diverse families. This will demonstrate your motivation to the team (which may, in turn, rub off on them) and enhance the skill set you bring to the table and your understanding of next steps.

Addressing cultural barriers directly sets the stage for respectful, informative, and constructive interactions. As a result, your child will receive a plan that suits their specific needs, and you will have the proper resources to support them beyond the classroom.

Tips for a Tiptop Treatment Team

You are the Team Captain

As a parent, you are the main stakeholder. You are the one team member who feels the deepest sense of unwavering commitment to treatment planning oversight and overhaul (when needed). While the other team members are passionate about supporting your child, they may, at times, feel burned out by other tasks. Therefore, they may require a bit of motivation from you, their team "captain."

In situations when more oversight and motivation are needed, or an overall change is necessary, you can step up in many different ways. Here are a few examples:

If you feel...	**Then try connecting with the team by...**
interventions do not align with your child's needs	■ revisiting your child's needs, treatment goals, and interventions to ensure there is clear alignment. ■ asking if the interventions are rooted in evidence and exactly what the expected outcomes are in terms of your child.
one or more team members are not following through with their responsibilities	■ clearly outlining details around roles and responsibilities (who/what/when/where/how). ■ being inquisitive and seeking to understand what is preventing them from following through, and what the team can do to help them move past it.
disjointed as a team	■ requesting periodic check-ins so the team can address the effectiveness of communication methods and progress monitoring, and any issues around exclusionary behaviors and team cohesion. ■ pausing to reflect on team member communication styles, approaches to the plan, organizational styles, and any other uniquely personal element that impacts the team dynamic.

If you feel...	Then try connecting with the team by...
there is too much problem-focused and deficit-based conversations	■ guiding the conversation into more solutions-focused and strengths-based angles by asking: What is going well? What is working? Was there a time when this issue did not occur? Where do we want my child to be in terms of this goal by the end of the year? Using this information, what can we change in order to get there?

As the main stakeholder and captain of the treatment team, you have the opportunity to come into planning meetings with an unmatched advantage and ability to inspire your fellow team members. If you're asking yourself, how so? The answer lies in your uniquely intimate and comprehensive vantage point. You have a 360-degree understanding of your child and, with a bit of research, the treatment planning process. You bring to the table something that no treatment provider can bring. That power enables you to move treatment planning mountains.

You can take full advantage of your position to build a treatment "dream team." Here are a few ways you can make this happen:

- **Prepare yourself.** Preparation is one of the most beneficial tasks you can do (see Chapter 6). It involves researching and educating yourself on the treatment process in your school district, on your child's disability or condition, and on potential treatment methodologies. This also means organizing your thoughts by writing down questions and ideas, important notes about your child, and requesting all documentation prior to the meeting so you can include any additional thoughts that may be helpful and speed up the process.

- **Come in with a "team player" mentality.** Adopt a collaborative mindset. This means actively building positive relationships with other team members, listening with an open mind, clearly expressing your thoughts, sharing information about your child to connect to any team members who may not know them, and providing/receiving purposeful feedback. In addition, being a team player means feeling safe to disagree and participating in solutions-focused counterarguments. You can continue to develop respectful and constructive relationships by approaching uncomfortable conversations with curiosity and confidence rather than avoidance or defensiveness.
- **Consider the players before crafting a playbook.** Before you can develop a plan for effective partnerships, you need to first understand your team. You can do this by showing genuine curiosity in your team members. Ask them to describe their roles and responsibilities at the school, if they have experience assisting children who have a profile similar to your child, and what you can do to support them. Pay attention to how they communicate in and out of the meeting room. What is their level of confidence and engagement in face-to-face meetings? Do

they engage more with emails, handwritten notes, or calls? Do they seem to be more passive, aggressive, assertive, or a combination of styles? Which type of communication style do they seem most responsive to? Use this information to guide your interactions.

Like every team effort, the effectiveness of your child's treatment team is dependent on the four Cs: communication, collaboration, consistency, and the commitment of its members. Mutual engagement, respect, and cooperation help maintain the four Cs. By using the strategies and tips outlined in this chapter, you can proactively work toward fostering and creating the treatment team of your dreams.

When FAPE Is Not Being Provided

Although rare, there can be situations where all efforts to ensure your child receives fair and appropriate support are in vain. If you find yourself having to fight for your child's rights, there are steps you can take to resolve disputes and get your child the support they are entitled to. The steps vary slightly between IEP and 504 services.

Before Filing a Formal Complaint

In many school districts, parents are first directed to consult with an **ombudsman**. Typically appointed by the state or local board of education, this neutral party provides free and confidential guidance. An advocate for a fair process, an ombudsman is a reliable resource to use before taking formal action. To find out if your district has appointed an ombudsman, contact your local board of education or search your district's website (under "parent resources" or "dispute resolution" tabs within the *Special Education* page).

Some districts also offer the option of a **Facilitated IEP**. This means either the superintendent of special education or a trained, neutral representative attends and facilitates an IEP meeting between you and the school. This representative then objectively observes and gathers information in order to propose possible resolutions.

Other districts offer the option of referring your complaint to a neutral third party for what is commonly called an **Administrative Review** or **Complaint Unit**. This group, usually tied to the district compliance office, investigates your complaint and responds with proposed resolutions within a specified time frame (usually fifteen to forty-five days).

Following, or in place of these options, **mediation** can be the next step in resolving disagreements. Offered as a free, neutral, and impartial final resort before due process, mediation is typically facilitated by an administrative law judge or someone with similar credentials employed by an independent state agency. Mediation usually occurs within thirty days of the request. The option is voluntary, and all parties must agree to participate.

Mediation serves the purpose of clarifying issues, allowing for open and safe dialogue, and guiding negotiations that serve all parties while keeping the focus on what's best for your child. Request forms for mediation and all other informal resolution options can be found on your school district's website.

All of these options are helpful if your goals include:

- Resolving relatively minor disputes
- Preserving positive relationships between all parties involved
- Gaining knowledge on how to work collaboratively with these parties in the future
- Avoiding the strain of a due process hearing

*NOTE: If your child has a 504 Plan and does not have an IEP, the next steps may vary based on your state. For more information on the process for violations related to Section 504, contact your school board.

When Informal Attempts Fail: Due Process

In some cases, disagreements and concerns cannot be resolved through non-formal avenues. Some may even be so flagrant that they require immediate escalation. These cases will go through due process.

The due process experience is similar to a trial case where both parties present arguments, evidence, and witnesses before an impartial hearing officer who then issues a decision. These hearings have been put in place by IDEA in order to resolve conflicts related to:

- **Identification** – disputes surrounding the diagnosis, or lack thereof, or disputes surrounding whether or not a child is identified for Child Find
- **Evaluation** – disagreements around the denial of, or the results of, an evaluation

- **Placement** – issues regarding educational placement
- **FAPE** – disagreements related to services, or lack thereof, and appropriateness of your child's IEP

To begin the process, you need to send a written request to both your state education department and school district within two years of the date that the violation occurred (or when you should have become aware that it occurred). This request must include your child's name and address, your child's school, concise details of the concerns and violations that have led to this request, and your proposed solutions to address and resolve these issues. You may also choose to include federal and state codes that you believe have been violated.

*NOTE: Carefully review your state's requirements for the complaint, as failure to include all necessary elements could lead to an "insufficiency objection." This would require edits to your complaint and could halt the process.

When your complaint is received, the school has ten days to draft a written response to address the violations claimed, as well as fifteen days to schedule and hold a **resolution session**.

*NOTE: Due to the "stay put" provision, your child will remain in their setting unless both parties agree that changes need to be made during due process.

A resolution session is where all parties first come together following a due process complaint. This final effort to resolve issues before a hearing allows both parties the opportunity to detail and respond to complaints and agree upon legally binding possible resolutions. This session allows you to voice your concerns with absolute certainty that the other party will listen with open minds, as no one wants to endure the lengthy, pricey, and arduous experience of a hearing. As such, you want to be sure you...

- Speak to the violations, as recognized by the law, rather than speaking from your emotions and frustrations caused by these potential violations.
- Come prepared with a clear and articulate argument, as well as potential resolutions.
- Address the violations, as opposed to attacking those who you believe performed the violations.
- Get everything in writing, including attendees, point/counterpoints, and decisions.
- Listen to the school's responses and avoid responding out of frustration.
- Come with an open mind focused on resolutions.

*NOTE: Unless waived by both parties to expedite the process, a resolution session is required when a complaint is filed by the family. However, this stage is not required if the school filed the complaint.

Using the resolution meeting discussion as a guide, the school will have a thirty-day "resolution period" in which they can attempt to resolve the issues raised. If they are unsuccessful, then a **pre-hearing conference** will be conducted.

*NOTE: Attorneys will not be present in the resolution session. However, if you choose to include your legal representative, the school then has the right to include theirs.

Following the resolution period, the administrative law judge assigned to your case will schedule a pre-hearing conference. This conference serves to ensure the complaints made actually fall under due process, and all parties understand the complaints. The conference also determines who will represent each party, the hearing date, and the start time. During this conference, or at some point before the hearing, you will need to disclose the witnesses and evidence/exhibits that you will be presenting in the hearing. Be sure to read any procedural guidelines to ensure you know and follow required actions regarding witnesses and evidence.

*NOTE: While you have the right to represent yourself and your child in the hearing, it is important to know that the school will have legal representation. Additionally, the school has been through this process before, and you will have the burden of proof in this case. For these reasons, it is highly advised that you consult with a legal representative who is well-versed in special education law. Information regarding low- to no-cost options can be found in Chapter 4.

The due process hearing will take place within forty-five days of the resolution period's deadline. A hearing typically involves...

- A brief introductory recap of the case by the hearing officer.
- Opening statements by both parties.

  *As the filing party, you will make your statement first.

- Both parties making their cases (stating arguments, presenting evidence and exhibits, calling witnesses, etc.).

  *As the filing party, you will be the first to make your case.

- Cross-examinations, re-direct examinations, and counterarguments.
- Closing arguments and suggestions for remedies.

  *If desired, you may request closing arguments be made in writing.

Following the hearing, both parties may be required to write a **brief**. A brief summarizes the arguments and any laws that were or were not violated. This brief serves to help the hearing officer as they make final determinations. From there, a final decision in regard to the hearing will be made no later than forty-five days after the resolution period ends. Both parties then have the opportunity to appeal the decision to a state or federal court within thirty to ninety days. (Check your state laws to find the exact time frame within your district.)

*NOTE: If you are not provided one, request a copy of the hearing transcripts. This may be useful should an appeal take place.

Discussing Resolutions

When it comes to confronting your child's school with concerns, you can never be overly prepared. Whether it is an amicable and negotiations-based discussion or a formal and potentially adversarial discussion, you will need to come in with confidence and composure. At the very least, you will need to be as prepared as the school. Here is a checklist you can use to guide your preparations:

Have I...

- Made logistical arrangements to ensure I can attend meetings or hearings without feeling rushed, distracted, or stressed?
- Completed the necessary forms completely and saved copies before sending them to the appropriate parties?
- Organized, organized, and organized some more? From educational records and printouts of my communications with the school to concise summaries of my concerns, needs, and evidence to prove my child's needs are not being met, have I organized everything so that I am absolutely prepared to speak confidently and directly about any topics that may arise?
- Ensured that I understand the data? Measurements and assessments can be hard to figure out. Have I ensured I know what data is being presented in these assessments and measurements? Can I speak to the data points and counter any possible rebuttals that may be brought up regarding them?
- Received and provided all necessary documents/data to appropriate parties to ensure a productive discussion?
- Reviewed the special education and/or resolution page on my district's website for a list of low- to no-cost special education attorneys, if I should need one?

If I am going to a due process hearing, have I ALSO...

- Researched and collected all pieces of data and sought counsel from a variety of purposeful resources prior to making the decision to file?
- Consulted with a special education attorney prior to filing my complaint?
- Studied past due process hearings in my district, their outcomes, and what led to those outcomes?
- Reviewed the law as it relates to my child's needs and experience?
- Considered the cost (time, financial, emotional, and mental)?
- Reviewed timelines so I can plan accordingly?
- Developed a strong narrative using evidence and witnesses that explain exactly how the school has not met my child's needs and has denied them FAPE?
- Outlined the school's precise decision and reasoning so that I can counter their stance?
- Gathered ample, concrete, and indisputable evidence, as well as counter evidence, to prove my narrative?
- Spoken with the school's attorney about any potential evidence and exhibits the school and I will be using?
- Ensured my evidence directly serves a purpose?
- Developed an organizational strategy for quick retrieval of evidence and exhibits during the hearing?

- Made at least four copies of my evidence (for myself, the hearing officer, the school, and any witness who needs to view this evidence as they answer questions)?
- Used every resource at my disposal to develop a concise and reasonable plan for remediation?
- Ensured witnesses are prepared, they know the day/time of the hearing, they are available at that day/time, and they have been properly subpoenaed, if needed?
- Prepared my witness questions, possible cross-examination questions for the witnesses of the other party, and possible re-direct questions after the other party cross-examines my witnesses?
- Created an agenda of what I will present, when, and how?
- Mentally prepared for the overwhelming speed at which the process takes place (typically seventy-five days or less)?
- Created a list of strategies to keep my emotions from impacting my ability to present a strong case in the hearing?
- Mentally prepared for an appeal (either by me or the school, depending on the outcome of due process)?

Due Process Timeline

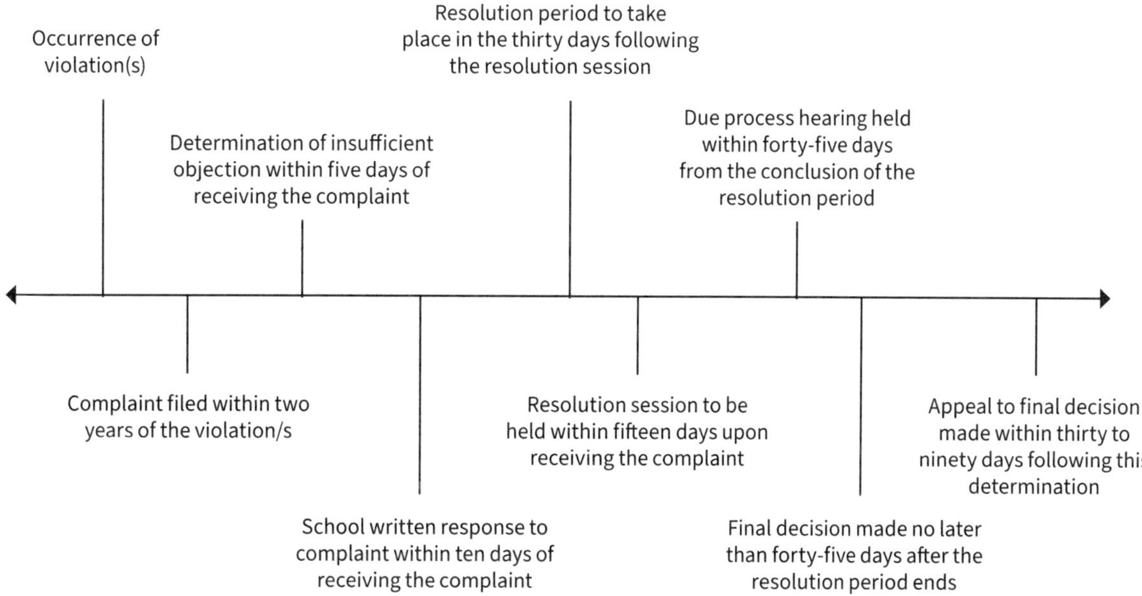

*NOTE: Exact times may vary. However, the entire process should take no more than seventy-five days from the filing of a complaint to the final decision. Refer to your state and district guidelines for concise time frames.

1. Murphy, A. N., & Risser, H. J. (2022). Perceived parent needs in engaging with therapeutic supports for children with disabilities in school settings: An exploratory study. *Research in Developmental Disabilities,* 123, 104183. https://doi.org/10.1016/j.ridd.2022.104183.
2. Weaver, A. D., & Ouye, J. C. (2015). A practical and research-based guide for improving IEP team meetings. (cover story). *Communique* (0164775X), 44(3), 1–25.
3. Bacon, J. K., & Causton-Theoharis, J. (2013). "It should be teamwork": A critical investigation of school practices and parent advocacy in special education. *International Journal of Inclusive Education,* 17, 682–699. doi:10.1080/13603116.2012.708060 [Taylor & Francis Online].
4. Francis, G. L., Blue-Banning, M., Haines, S. J., Turnbull, A. P., & Gross, J. M. S. (2016). Building "our school": Parental perspectives for building trusting family-professional partnerships. *Preventing School Failure: Alternative Education for Children, 60*(4), 329–336. https:// doi.org/10.1080/1045988X.2016.1164115.
5. Murphy, A. N., & Risser, H. J. (2022). Perceived parent needs in engaging with therapeutic supports for children with disabilities in school settings: An exploratory study. *Research in Developmental Disabilities,* 123, 104183. https://doi.org/10.1016/j.ridd.2022.104183.
6. Burke, M. M. (2013). Improving parental involvement: Training special education advocates. *Journal of Disability Policy Studies, 23*(4), 225–234. https://doi-org.proxy1.library.jhu.edu/10.1177/1044207311424910.

7. Fish, W. W. (2008). The IEP meeting: Perceptions of parents of students who receive special education services. *Preventing School Failure, 53*(1), 8-14. Retrieved from https://www.proquest.com/scholarly-journals/iep-meeting-perceptions-parents-students-who/docview/228569346/se-2.
8. Weaver and Ouye, "A Practical and Research-Based Guide."
9. Murphy and Risser, "Perceived Parent Needs."
10. Sanderson, K. A. (2023) "Be prepared to fight like hell": Parent advice for IEP meetings, *Exceptionality* DOI: 10.1080/09362835.2023.2184819.
11. Fish, "The IEP Meeting."
12. Bacon and Causton-Theoharis, "It Should Be Teamwork."
13. Sanderson, "Be Prepared to Fight."
14. Dunn, C., Gilson, C., & Yllades, V. (2022). Experiences of Latinx immigrant parents of children with developmental disabilities in the IEP process. *Education and Training in Autism and Developmental Disabilities, 57*(4), 404–416.
15. Ibid.
16. Murphy and Risser, "Perceived Parent Needs."
17. Park, J., Turnbull, A. P., & Park, H.S. (2001). Quality of partnerships in service provision for Korean American parents of children with disabilities: A qualitative inquiry. *Journal of the Association for Persons with Severe Handicaps, 26*(3), 158–170. https://doi.org/10.2511/rpsd.26.3.158.
18. Rossetti, Z., Redash, A., Sauer, J.S., Oanh, B., Wen, Y., & Regensburger, D. (2020). Access, accountability, and advocacy: Culturally and linguistically diverse families' participation in IEP meetings. *Exceptionality,* 28:4, 243-258, DOI: 10.1080/09362835.2018.1480948.
19. Wolfe, K., & Durán, L. K. (2013). Culturally and linguistically diverse parents' perceptions of the IEP process. *Multiple Voices for Ethnically Diverse Exceptional Learners, 13*(2), 4–18. https://doi.org/10.56829/muvo.13.2.y452140732mlg231.
20. Murphy and Risser, "Perceived Parent Needs."
21. Park, Turnbull, and Park, "Quality of Partnerships."
22. Rossetti, et al., "Access, Accountability, and Advocacy."
23. Wolfe and Durán, "Culturally and Linguistically Diverse Parents."
24. Rossetti, et al., "Access, Accountability, and Advocacy."
25. Park, Turnbull, and Park, "Quality of Partnerships."
26. Wolfe and Durán, "Culturally and Linguistically Diverse Parents."
27. Ibid.
28. Park, Turnbull, and Park, "Quality of Partnerships."

CHAPTER 8

Your Voice Matters: How to Ensure You Are Heard

This chapter is dedicated to you – the most important person in your child's life!

The strategies and evidence-based practices described on the following pages can help you ease family stress, reignite your passion, and rejuvenate your mind and body without feeling guilt or shame.

Parenting a child with a disability or condition can be exhausting yet exhilarating, frustrating yet freeing, disheartening yet encouraging, and frightening yet soothing. When riding this emotional roller coaster, you may put your needs on the backburner, but that can lead to a cycle of compassion fatigue and hinder the quality of care you provide.

Easing Your Stress at Home

While rewarding and remarkably fulfilling, raising a child with a disability comes with many stressors. The demands on your time and energy may feel overwhelming, your preferred parenting style and approach may have to change, and the finances needed to provide care, including specialized childcare, may feel crushing. Pressures like these can lead to rapid and profound compassion fatigue or burnout. Studies show that parents experiencing distress oftentimes disregard their need for self-care and support.[1]

It is vital that you purposefully and consistently engage in self-care and compassion practices. Allowing yourself moments to reignite and reset will, in turn, allow you to maintain the health, strength, and overall vitality of your family. Here are several evidence-based parenting practices that can help reduce your stress:

- **Mindful Parenting.** Known to reduce parental stress and increase overall positivity in parent-child interactions, this technique involves slowing down and being in the present.[2] Mindful-based strategies can help you reduce judgment, increase self- and environmental awareness, and avoid reactionary responses to distressing situations. Mindful parenting techniques include...
    - ▷ Breathing slowly and creating a calm energy before responding to stressful situations.
    - ▷ Being aware of your emotions, as well as the emotions of your child, in moments of high stress.
    - ▷ Practicing acceptance and gratitude.
    - ▷ Listening to your child, actively and intentionally, without judgment so they feel heard and seen.

- **Emotion-Oriented Coping.** When distressing situations elevate your emotions, use strategies that can calm you, such as...
    - ▷ Practicing meditation to slow your breathing, body, and mind.
    - ▷ Journaling to get thoughts out of your head and onto paper so you can dissect your distress and focus on positive, solution-oriented options.
    - ▷ Learning the art of absolute forgiveness and radical acceptance.
    - ▷ Taking part in stress-reduction activities that work for you, such as nature walks, time with friends, or a warm bath.
- **Specialized Parent Support Groups.** Connecting with other parents who are caring for children with similar needs can be a source of strength and community. These groups sometimes involve wellness activities, such as equine-assisted therapy, art, or nature hikes. They also can simply be spaces that allow parents to relax and recharge together. These bonding experiences have been shown to reduce feelings of isolation, stress, and worry.

Self-Care, Physical Wellness, and Emotional Well-Being

Your quality of life can be negatively affected when you fail to care for your own psychological and physical needs.

Studies show that a parent's efficacy (belief in their parenting skills and feeling like a competent caretaker) closely correlate to psychological wellness.[3] Unfortunately, many parents of children with disabilities or other conditions often carry with them feelings of guilt and grief, as well as a lower sense of being able to perform their parental role successfully.[4] Moreover, they are twice as likely to suffer from physical ailments, such as headaches and sleep deprivation, than parents of non-disabled children.[5]

Tending to your own needs does not have to be daunting or time-consuming, nor should it feel selfish or shameful. With a bit of reflection, planning, and dedication, you can easily adopt self-care routines into your life to alleviate the stressors that zap your health.

Reflection should be the first (and a continuous) step in your self-care and wellness routine. Start by reflecting on your goals:

- *What is missing from my life?*
- *What do I need that I'm not receiving?*
- *How do I feel about self-care and compassion in general? Do I have any preconceived notions or have negative associations with the concept?*
- *What barriers kept me from tending to my own needs in the past? How can I overcome these barriers moving forward?*
- *What emotions, thoughts, and physical responses am I experiencing more frequently than I would like?*

Use your responses to those questions to create concrete goals or intentions you hope to achieve through dedicated self-care and compassion practices. Once you are comfortable with the reflection step, think about what you know about self-care and compassion. For example...

- *What kinds of practices have you explored in the past? Which were most beneficial for you?*
- *Where can you obtain more information specifically related to your personal goals or intentions?*
- *What resources are available to you (webinars, local therapeutic groups, local Meetup groups, websites, etc.)?*

Once you have set your goals or intentions and have created an index of resources, think of ways to put self-care and compassion practices into your daily life. Your self-care and compassion plan will be similar to finding the right treatment plan for your child. It takes time, commitment, and a few adjustments before it can fully meet your needs. Begin by identifying where your life feels most out of balance.

- *What areas in your life feel most neglected – spirituality, physical wellness, personal and intellectual growth, socializing, family relationships, career, or emotional nourishment?*
- *What do you feel is missing from the most neglected areas of your life?*
- *How much time can you devote to nourishing these areas every day? Every week? Every month?*

- *What is one daily practice you can incorporate to nourish these parts of your life? When do you intend to do this practice each day?*
- *What is one long-term (not a daily practice) change you can work toward to nourish these areas of your life?*

Reigniting Your Energy

As described earlier, different stages of the treatment planning process can bring up different emotions that can be daunting and draining.

As a loving, protective parent, your instincts may be to take a "full-steam ahead" approach, pushing yourself while running on nothing but fumes. This is understandable. You want what is best for your child and won't rest until you are certain they are in a good place. However, it is essential you have a full physical and emotional tank during the initial stages of the treatment planning process.

Caring for Yourself While Being an Effective Advocate

Advocating for your child is a key part of being a parent. While you may not be as experienced with treatment plans as others on your child's team, you are the one person who knows your child best. You understand who they are and what would benefit them the most. For this reason, your voice commands respect.

However, the role of advocate can be challenging. Even when working with a treatment plan dream team, advocating can be a long and taxing battle. This is par-

FIGURE 11

The Path to Success: Stages a Parent May Experience

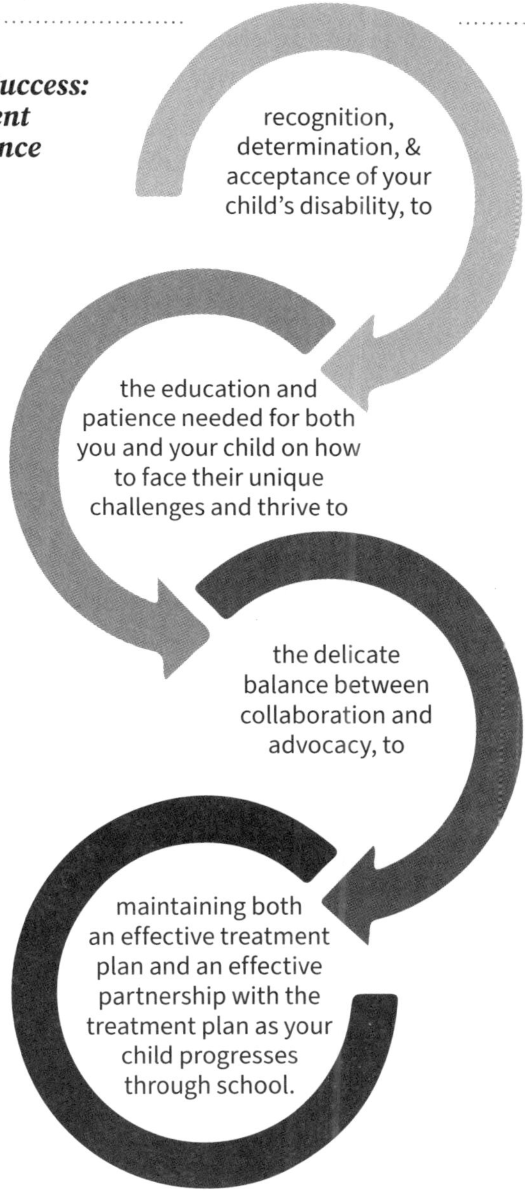

ticularly true in the initial stages of diagnoses and the creation of a treatment plan. Reasons that can undermine your ability to be an effective advocate include:

- **The pain of hearing conversations about the diagnosis and accepting an individualized plan.** Regardless of your level of acceptance as it relates to your child's diagnosis or condition, it can be hurtful and angering to hear others discuss your child's struggles. This can be particularly challenging in a treatment planning meeting where discussions may feel cold and rushed.
- **Stress and high emotions.** Studies indicate that parents, when advocating for their child, often feel high levels of stress, anger, and other intense negative emotions regardless of how friendly and supportive their child's treatment team may be.
- **Family, marital, and career stress.** Parents who are advocating for their children often experience higher levels of stress within the family. Issues, such as time and the emotional weight spent on research and advocacy, can take its toll on family relationships, marital happiness, and career. In a two-person household, issues may also arise when one parent feels as if they are advocating more than the other or feels unsupported.
- **Imposter syndrome or feeling like an outsider in the system.** Typically, the majority of individuals involved in the treatment planning process are educators and other professionals who engage in the treatment process regularly. This can lead parents to feel like outsiders, imposters, or even inadequate.

All of these challenges can be reduced by incorporating small but powerful actions into your daily routine throughout the treatment planning process. Start by reflecting on both your schedule and your mindset:

- *Are my schedule and mindset controlled and organized, or chaotic and disorderly?*
- *Have I set aside planned time to think about my advocacy role, or have I let those thoughts occupy all of my time?*

If your schedule feels chaotic and your thoughts are fixated on the treatment planning process, work at finding a balance to avoid burning out physically and emotionally. Regardless of how accepting and understanding you are of your child's diagnosis or condition, it can still sting to hear others discuss your child in that light. Consider how you will respond if this happens during the treatment planning meeting, as well as how you will respond in moments of perceived tension.

- *What words or voice tones could be triggering for you?*
- *How would those triggers impact you physically, mentally, behaviorally, and emotionally?*
- *Will your emotions impact your ability to participate in a fully present and clear-minded way?*
- *If this becomes an issue during the meeting, how can you move past it?*

Mindful breathing, sipping a warm drink, shifting to alternative and more positive thoughts, or repeating a mantra to yourself can be very helpful when feelings of defensiveness or stress arise. Finally, reflect on your role within the treatment planning team.

- *Do you recognize and fully trust the importance of your voice at the table?*
- *Do you allow "I'm an imposter" thoughts or feelings of inadequacy to impact your ability to advocate?*
- *Are you comfortable asking questions, pushing back, and jumping in when needed?*

Once you have reflected on how to manage and improve your actions and emotions, you can then focus on strengthening partnerships within the treatment team. This can increase your trust in the treatment planning process, ensure more positive collaboration, and strengthen your skills as an advocate. These outcomes will, in turn, reduce stress, negative emotions, and the likelihood of burnout.

A good first step to take when trying to strengthen partnerships so you can be a better advocate for your child is to become a volunteer. Offer to help in your child's school, volunteer to monitor lunch periods and recess, or offer to become a room parent. These volunteer opportunities can give you more insight into the way your child's classroom and school functions while simultaneously strengthening your relationships with important adults in your child's support network.

Another positive step can be sending periodic messages of appreciation via email to your child's teacher and other members of your child's support team. Recognizing their hard work can help you establish a connection and build positive relationships.

Lastly, continue to educate yourself on the role of advocate in the school setting. Read forums, attend workshops and webinars, review advocacy-centered websites, or ask the school to recommend any resources for you. Greater knowledge leads to greater confidence and emotional well-being.

Research and Reflection: Recommendations for Optimal Advocacy

As a key member on your child's treatment team, your advocacy skills will naturally improve with time and experience. However, a bit of additional effort will further enhance your ability to recognize and respond to obstacles that may arise. This extra effort may include researching the art of the treatment planning process and common hurdles that arise, practicing critical self-reflection to determine how you can be a more effective team member, or determining how to identify and use productive feedback in order to improve the process.

Using Research to Proactively Strengthen Advocacy and Team Member Skills

Research can be done in any number of ways. Your local library, internet searches, peer-reviewed educational journals, and reports in mainstream media can all be sources of information on the barriers and best practices of parent advocacy. You can even do your own research by speaking with local parents or posting questions on advocacy and parenting forums. Your local library also may provide free access to databases with links to research studies specifically related to parental experiences in the treatment planning process.

No matter the approach you prefer, the more reliable information you can gather regarding potential pitfalls can only improve your chances of avoiding them. For example, a number of studies and **online advocacy-focused websites** discuss common obstacles that can interfere with a parent's ability to effectively advocate and collaborate during the treatment planning process. One such study showed that common obstacles include a lack of opportunity for input, poor communication and organization during treatment planning meetings, systemic and demographic barriers, and a lack of empathy or recognition of parent emotions.[6]

Online Resources to Help You Become an Empowered Advocate

www.understood.org/en

www.parentcenterhub.org/find-your-center/

www.wrightslaw.com/blog/

https://adayinourshoes.com

Knowing those potential obstacles, start to proactively prepare by asking yourself:

- *How will I know if I'm encountering any of these obstacles?*
- *What strategies can help me minimize or overcome each obstacle?*
- *How prepared am I emotionally, and do I have the skills necessary to overcome these obstacles?*

For additional insights, see **Figure 12**.

Using Reflection to Proactively Strengthen Advocacy and Team Member Skills

Critical self-reflection involves recognizing and challenging one's own interpretations and assumptions, being aware of one's strengths and areas of growth, and making sense of things based on experience, knowledge, and exploration of thought. Critical self-reflection enables you to become attuned with your own thoughts, judgments, and preconceived ideas. Once you gain this awareness, you then have the power to shift your thoughts, as needed, in order to become a more open-minded and effective team player.

Critical self-reflection also enables you to become more attuned to your own aptitude and areas of growth. This, in turn, can increase the confidence you have in your abilities and unlock opportunities to set goals and overcome challenges. In addition, you can better understand yourself within the context of the treatment team.

FIGURE 12

What is the obstacle?	How will I know if I am encountering this obstacle?
Lack of opportunity for input	■ Being talked over or talked through ■ No pause to ask for my thought ■ I will feel more like a viewer than a participant
Poor communication and organization	■ Time not being used effectively ■ Not provided with the necessary materials ■ Attendees seem confused about the agenda
Systemic and demographic barriers	■ Not provided an interpreter
Lack of empathy for parent emotions	■ Only sharing negatives and deficiencies ■ Cold atmosphere

Strategies to help me reduce obstacles.	Areas for personal growth.
■ Come prepared with talking points that I want to cover ■ Ask the team to slow down	■ Imposter fears ■ Too reserved and may hold back as a result
■ Proactively request an agenda and necessary documents ahead of the meeting ■ Ensure I get my full allocated time	■ Again, too reserved which may prevent me from speaking up
■ Refuse to meet until an interpreter is present	■ Not applicable
■ Managing my own emotions ■ Sharing more about who my child is	■ Will be hard to be more objective or take emotions off the table

As an advocate and member of your child's treatment team, you should intentionally carve out time to actively practice critical self-reflection on your role and your performance in that role. Ideally, this dedicated time would occur after interactions with the team. You could even reflect with a trusted friend or write your thoughts in a reflection journal or e-journal.

Here are some suggested questions you can ask yourself during self-reflection:

Questions Before a Team Interaction:

1. *What do I hope to accomplish as an advocate for my child?*
2. *What specific skills do I need in order to be an effective advocate?*
3. *What skills do I feel most comfortable and confident using?*
4. *What skills am I lacking or unsure about?*
5. *What assumptions do I have about the school and the members of my child's team?*
6. *What assumptions do I have about the treatment planning process?*

Questions Following a Team Interaction:

1. *What was this experience like? What happened to make me feel this way?*
2. *What did I do or not do to encourage growth, teamwork, and effective action?*

3. *What did others do or not do to encourage growth, teamwork, and effective action?*
4. *What knowledge or skills did I show or use during the experience?*
5. *What knowledge or skills were missing from my performance during this experience?*
6. *How did this experience impact my understanding and knowledge of advocacy and team collaboration?*
7. *What new knowledge and understanding did I gain? How can I continue to gain new knowledge and understanding?*
8. *Why is this understanding and knowledge important?*
9. *What can I do with this information to grow in my role?*

The Role of Feedback

Meaningful feedback allows us to gain a perspective that may otherwise go unnoticed. Too often, we are unable to recognize our own strengths or areas that require improvement. So, who can you go to for trusted feedback? The members of your child's treatment team, parents who have children with special needs, and any support personnel you work with, such as an educational advocate or child therapist, can all be options.

Before asking for feedback from team members, parents, or other supportive experts, ask yourself:

- *Have I prepared myself emotionally to receive criticism?*

- *Am I aware of the communication style of the person I'm seeking feedback from in order to avoid misinterpretations or unnecessary distress?*
- *Do I have a set of clear "asks" to ensure the feedback is guided by my own needs and wants?*
- *How can I stop the feedback or conversation if I need to pause for reflection or clarification?*

As you gather information or feedback from others regarding your role, it is important to recognize what is helpful and lends itself to growth and what is unnecessary or unhelpful. When analyzing feedback from your teammates and peers, consider the following:

- *What did I learn from this conversation?*
- *What, if any, feedback was unhelpful or triggering?*
- *Using this information, what steps can I take to grow?*
- *Should I follow up with this person to brainstorm growth steps and/or gather appropriate resources?*
- *How else can I use this feedback?*

Conclusion

Caring for a child with a disability or other condition can, at times, feel overwhelming. However, with the structures and supports enacted by our government and educational system, you should never feel stuck in hopelessness and despair.

Throughout your child's development, you will have a strong and skilled team by your side, guiding you in moments of confusion and ensuring your child achieves on every front. With a bit of flexibility, consistency, resiliency, assertiveness, and care, you can feel confident that you are giving your child everything they need to achieve greatness.

1. Miller, A. E., Green, T. D., & Lambros, K. M. (2019). Foster parent self-care: A conceptual model. *Children and Youth Services Review, 99,* 107–114. https://doi.org/10.1016/j.childyouth.2019.01.014.
2. Kakhki, Z. B., Mashhadi, A., Yazdi, S. A. A., & Saleh, S. (2022). The effect of mindful parenting training on parent–child interactions, parenting stress, and cognitive emotion regulation in mothers of preschool children. *Journal of Child and Family Studies, 31*(11), 3113–3124. https://doi.org/10.1007/s10826-022-02420-z.
3. Ho, M. Y., & Liang, S. (2021). Emotion-oriented coping and parental competency: An evidence-based parenting intervention for parents of children with special educational needs. *Child & Family Social Work, 26*(4), 518–529. https://doi.org/10.1111/cfs.12834.
4. Rahayu, W. F., & Mangunsong, F. M. (2020). Parenting self-efficacy mediates the effect of parental acceptance on the social-emotional abilities of children with special needs. *Life Span and Disability, 23*(2), 211-238.
5. Panczykowski, H., Murphy, L., Heyward, K., & Hupp, T. (2022). Lived experiences of parents of children with disabilities engaged in a support group incorporating equines. *Research in Developmental Disabilities,* 128, 104294–104294. https://doi.org/10.1016/j.ridd.2022.104294.
6. Weaver, A. D., & Ouye, J. C. (2015). A practical and research-based guide for improving IEP team meetings. (cover story). *Communique* (0164775X), 44(3), 1–25.

APPENDIX

Key Definitions to Remember in Treatment Planning

Accommodation: Slight changes made to the learning environment (setting, timing, response, format, presentation, etc.) that do not impact the content learned. Typically included in treatments, such as 504 Plans, accommodations remove barriers to a youth's ability to learn and show what they have learned. Some examples include extended time to complete assignments and tests, materials provided in primary language, frequent breaks, proximity seating, reduced distractions, or breaking assignments into smaller, manageable chunks.

Activities of Daily Living (ADL): Activities that are necessary for daily functioning, such as eating, grooming/hygiene, and toileting.

Adequate Yearly Progress (AYP): Accountability measures that capture student achievement through various testing modalities. A product of the No Child Left Behind Act of 2001, all students are expected to demonstrate progress toward, and meet at least the minimal requirements of, core content area goals as determined by the state and/or district.

Annual Goal: A measurable and achievable objective or statement written into an IEP identifying the skill/ behavior a student is expected to demonstrate within a certain period of time.

Annual Review: A required yearly meeting where the team involved in treatment planning and implementation (professionals, caretakers, and other supports) gathers to review and discuss progress toward goals, determine next steps, and make adjustments as needed to ensure maximum gains are made.

Behavior Intervention Plan/Behavior Management Plan (BIP/BMP): Created by the school IEP team or select members of the team, this plan includes observations and analysis to determine behavior needs and goals. It also includes supplementary aids, modifications, and progress tracking to ensure children are placed in the least restrictive environment (LRE).

Child Find: A mandate of IDEA, this law requires districts to search for and evaluate all youth (early infancy to age 21) suspected of having, or do have, a disability (regardless of degree or severity) that could require special education services.

Continuum of Alternative Placement: An educational setting determined to be the best option when needs cannot be met in a traditional classroom. This setting may include another classroom, another school, home school, a hospital, an institution, or another setting that provides necessary supports.

Early Childhood Intervention: Programs designed to assist and support children younger than school-age.

English Language Learner/English as a Second Language/Limited English Proficiency (ELL/ESL/LEP): A child who is learning the English language, who has learned it but resides in an environment where there is another dominant language, or who is not yet at proficiency of the language to where they can maintain grade level objectives in an English-only classroom.

Due Process: As the guardians of a youth who has specialized services and/or treatment plans, parents/caretakers have certain rights, known as due process. These rights are one formal approach to resolving any disputes regarding special education, such as disagreements, negligence in following through with treatment plans, etc.

Extended School Year Services (ESY): Youth receiving special education services may be eligible for supports that extend beyond the normal school year. These supports vary greatly, depending on student needs. ESY eligibility is typically determined during the annual review.

Family Education Rights and Privacy Act (FERPA): Legislation that requires all educational institutions receiving federal funds to protect the privacy of youth. Any identifiable information, such as treatment plans and special services received, must remain private. Access to and release of any of this information is strictly governed.

Functional Behavior Assessment (FBA): Created in alignment with a BIP/BMP, this solutions-focused inquiry identifies targeted unhealthy and undesired behaviors, antecedents and triggers to those negative behaviors, and possible interventions to reduce those behaviors.

Individualized Family Service Plan (IFSP): Plans developed in early childhood (sometimes known as infancy and toddler plans) that outline interventions for youth with disabilities and their families. The plans typically involve goals outlined by the team (family, service provider, and a service coordinator) that set the stage for entering the school years.

Informed Consent: A requirement set forth through IDEA, this signed agreement of a parent/caretaker must be obtained before evaluations, revisions to plans, or termination of plans can occur.

Interventions: Specific, focused, and purposeful procedures used to support youth who need additional reinforcements in academic, social, emotional, and overall life skills attainment.

Least Restrictive Environment (LRE): Brought forth through IDEA, LRE mandates that educational institutions teach youth with disabilities in a general education setting with appropriate aids and supplements to the maximum extent possible.

Mediation: A step typically taken before due process, mediation is a means for resolving conflict and/or disagreements regarding special education services. The hopes of mediation are that all parties involved can come to an agreement together, rather than having to go through the judicial process.

Modification: Adjustments to the manner, content, extent, and presentation requirements that are used to demonstrate mastery of a concept. Examples can include shortening the length of an assignment, altering the assignment, or changing the way a youth is graded on assignments and projects.

Other Health Impairment (OHI): A chronic disability or acute illness that impacts learning and therefore qualifies a child for special education services.

Present Level of Performance (PLOP, PLP): A description of skills, abilities, challenges, and any other pertinent information at the time that a treatment plan is developed. This provides a baseline for creating goals.

Related Services: Any additional developmental or corrective services required for a youth to fully access and benefit from special education. Examples include transportation, speech and language, occupational therapy, or psychological services.

Response to Intervention (RTI): A method for identifying youth who may need additional supports, RTI systematically assesses progress and monitors the effectiveness of supports in place. This is an alternative to special education, but it does not include the safety of a legally binding plan.

Specific Learning Disability: One or more disabilities or conditions that impact a child's ability to process, understand, or learn. This could include difficulties with speaking, writing, listening, performing calculations, reading, or spelling.

Supplementary Aids and Services: Built for use in a general education setting, these aids and services remove barriers that may hinder access to education. Examples include access to assistive technology, large print, modified assignments, or behavioral support.

Triennial Review: A required meeting that takes place every three years at which time the team involved in treatment planning and implementation (professionals, caretakers, and other supports) determines if a youth is still eligible for specialized services and plans.

Landmark Decisions in the Educational System

Individuals with Disabilities Education Act (IDEA)	■ Guarantees all youth ages 3 to 21 receive free and appropriate education in a least restrictive environment ■ Encourages parent and student voices in decision-making ■ Outlines eligibility for services and accommodations in an IEP plan ■ Ensures procedural rights of students with disabilities and their families are enforced
Americans with Disabilities Act (ADA)	■ Civil rights law that prohibits discrimination against individuals with disabilities or impairments in federally funded programs ■ Ensures reasonable accommodations for individuals with physical, mental, and learning disabilities or impairments ■ Protects the rights of students and employees (such as educators)
Section 504 of the Rehabilitation Act of 1973	■ Ensures individuals with impairments that substantially impact daily life are provided with reasonable accommodations and modifications that allow them equal access as their peers ■ Individuals must be "otherwise qualified" for the program or activity in order to be protected under this act

Every Student Succeeds Act (ESSA)	■ Replaced "No Child Left Behind" in 2015 ■ Provides access to college-ready curriculum for all students ■ Ensures proper supports and high standards for disadvantaged and high-need students ■ Requires educator accountability and ownership of student achievement

Key Agencies, Offices, and Organizations at a Glance

United States Department of Education (USDOE)	■ Regulates federal education policy and law ■ Presides over research related to national education and identifies key findings ■ Ensures equal access to education for all
Office of Civil Rights (OCR)	■ A sub-agency within the USDOE ■ Regulates federal education policy and legislation ■ Implements civil rights laws in education ■ Prevents discrimination in education ■ Enforces HIPAA (Health Insurance Portability and Accountability Act) to ensure privacy is protected
Office of Special Education and Rehabilitative Services (OSERS)	■ Overseas two key programs: Office of Special Education Programs (OSEP) and Rehabilitation Services Agency (RSA) ■ Develops, implements, and monitors policy and legislation that directly impacts individuals with disabilities ■ Provides leadership and support to state and local agencies related to FAPE and LRE

Council for Exceptional Children (CEC)	■ Largest international professional organization aimed at improving outcomes for individuals with disabilities, gifts, and those who are twice exceptional ■ Advocates, builds partnerships, and provides professional development for educators working with exceptional students

INDEX

D

E

F

G

H

I

U